The Con Club

CW01636678

Hello Ian

Thank you for everything that you do. It is So important.

Best Wishes

Keith.

KEITH DAVID McCOY

Edited by Charlie Wilson
Cover and Interior design by Steve Mead Graphic Design

Ebook: 978-1-9163652-6-1
Paperback: 978-1-9163652-7-8

This is dedicated to all those who dream and hope, and do their best minute to minute, hour to hour, day to day, to make their lives, the lives of those around them, and the world a better place. Well done and thank you.

Rotten Luck

1

The Smiths are an average couple. There is nothing special or unusual about them. Some of their neighbours view them as normal, others as bland. Derek Smith works as a bookkeeper. Years ago, he took some accountancy exams, but he failed his finals and never got round to resitting them. He agreed with his wife, Gertrude, that he would take a year out to support her as she was about to give birth and then would of course pass them at a later date, but they ended up with twins, so! As well as that, Gertrude suffered with what is now widely known as postpartum depression. At the time she was viewed as a woman who was easily stressed out and always tired, someone who'd had a much too romantic notion of what having children would be like and as a result was very underprepared and then struggled to cope.

Following a phone call this evening, the Smiths, without breaking the speed limit, rush to their local Accident and Emergency department: their son Ted has been involved in an accident. They don't wait to read the rules, written in small print, regarding paying for parking, and as a result on departure they'll have to pay a fine. It's one of those setups where you have to pay in advance, for either one hour, two hours, three hours or over four. They don't bother with all this as their only focus when they arrive is Ted.

Their other son, Mike, is there already. He has spoken with a receptionist, and when his parents arrive, he is able to take them to a waiting area. Stressed out and shocked, he briefs them on everything he's learnt in the ten minutes that he spent there prior to them turning up.

Ted is in a critical state; he is being operated on. He was out for a jog and was hit by a car. The car didn't stop. Another car was passing, and the female driver saw what had happened. She did stop, and dialled 999 and asked for an ambulance. Ted was unconscious. The woman, who had done a health and safety course at work, knew how to apply pressure where blood was exiting the body, and also knew how to do CPR. There was no need for CPR, though, as Ted was breathing. There were lots of cuts and grazes, a twisted leg that looked broken, but no obvious blood loss. However, internally there was damage to his liver and other blood vessels, which meant Ted's blood pressure was dangerously low. He had also sustained a terrible bang to the head, and even though his skull wasn't broken, there were cracks that the female first aider couldn't see. There was blood leaking from his ear, as well as brain fluid, and these weren't being held back as his eardrum was also perforated.

The medical team are under huge pressure to save Ted. There are two consultant surgeons working on him, as well as junior doctors, senior nurses and junior nurses, with every person knowing their role and working in strong synchronisation, just as if they were all in a beehive. They are able to give Ted four pints of blood, and also slow the leakage from the liver, but they can't completely stop it. Then the neurological damage he sustained leads to seizures, and his torso arches upwards and his head backwards. The fitting increases the damage to his brain, starving it of ever more much needed oxygen. This all culminates in a cardiac arrest, and it is this that finishes him off and will end up on his death certificate as the cause of death. The team tried so hard to save him, but even if they had managed to get his heart working again, the liver damage would have ended him within twenty-four hours anyway, and his brain was so badly damaged too that even if the liver had been fine, he most likely would have had to spend the rest of his life in a brain injury unit.

Once the team agree he is deceased and there is no more they can do for him, most of the medics leave Ted; they are needed elsewhere. Only a nurse and a healthcare assistant remain, to tidy him up a little. They wash his face, brush his hair, and use a few very large skin-coloured plasters to cover the surgical incisions that were needed to access his liver. There is no point in suturing the wounds right now. What is needed in the here and now is for them to do their best to make him look as peaceful as possible, so as to try to limit the shock and pain his family will invariably experience when they come to spend some moments with his body.

Eventually, Ted is ready and the family are shown into the room where he has been laid out. Gertrude gasps for air as if she has fallen into ice-cold water and then becomes tearful and holds on to her deceased son's hand. It's starting to lose heat, and his skin has started to pale. She has only ever seen him this pale once before, ten years earlier, when as a fifteen-year-old he had terrible food poisoning. Eight rounds of vomiting and thirty bouts of diarrhoea in a twenty-four-hour period eventually necessitated a visit to this very hospital. She now starts to cry in a muted way.

Derek is in shock too and is standing on the opposite side of the bed. He looks down at Ted, but he doesn't touch him. Derek is utterly devastated, but he doesn't show it. He doesn't cry, and he says nothing, not a sound. He wants to hold it together, to support Gertrude. He has a sense that this is how his grandfather would have behaved if it was he who was at his deceased son's bedside. He tries to act like his grandfather a lot, as his grandfather was the family hero. He was a mechanic who serviced the fighter planes that defended Britain during the war; he was a man who just got on with things.

Mike is bawling, tears and snot, and he is at the bottom of the bed rubbing and hugging the feet and twisted lower legs of his identical twin.

After an hour, they realise that there is much that needs doing. They are advised that an autopsy will still need to take place, but that it's merely a formality, as the cause of death is clear. Afterwards, Ted will be taken to the hospital mortuary, and then the Smiths will need to organise moving him elsewhere, which in reality will be taken care of by whatever company they hire to manage the funeral arrangements. The details of companies that can do this are shared with the Smiths. Then they head home; that is, once they've paid the parking fine to the private company that won the tender to penalise those car owners who don't abide by the car park rules. Mike was angry and wanted to pick an argument with the car park company employee, but his father said nothing and just handed over his debit card, which was swiped, while Gertrude, with an expressionless face, looked into the distance, saying nothing. This is how she normally presents anyway, but on the inside, she is different now. Her normal internal architecture is one of being flat in mood and emotionless and this is still there. What's new is a deep, deep, dark hole that is full of despair.

2

The female driver who helped the injured Ted gives the police an account of what she witnessed including the make of the car. 'It was a vintage Aston Martin, just like in the old James Bond films. The same silver colour too.'

It turns out that the driver of the car was, and still is, drunk. The man isn't so drunk that he doesn't realise he knocked Ted over, he knows he did, but he also knows that he's fairly pissed and needs to get home as quickly as possible, sober up and then come up with a way to deny any involvement in the incident should the police be able to link him to it. And perhaps this might have worked out had he been able to chill behind the wheel and slow down his actions and thinking. Instead, he goes through a red light, and an officer in a passing police car sees this particular indiscretion and pulls him over.

The driver is pleasant in his conversation with the policeman, but he's slurring his words. His friend in the passenger seat comes across as more composed and nearly convinces the officer to let them go on their way, but the officer can see the driver's face is very red, despite him saying he's only had a tipple of sherry, and when the waft of alcohol hits the officer's olfactory senses, his professional integrity takes over and he calmly asks the driver to get out of the car. The driver can't walk in a straight line, but pleasantly complies when asked to blow into the breathalyser machine. He is over the limit. He is arrested and brought down to the station. His friend heads away in a taxi.

At the station, the drunk driver has blood taken (a few days later the results will show he was approximately four times over the legal limit). His solicitor attends the station shortly after, does the necessary and drives his client home.

The following day, it becomes apparent that the drunk driver's car is a match for the hit and run, and there is a dent on the left side of the car. The now-sober driver attends the station again, this time by appointment, in the company of his solicitor. He is charged with a number of things in relation to Ted. He doesn't make any comment; his solicitor deals with everything.

The local newspapers and social media report that a man has been charged in connection with the incident that led to Ted's death.

The Smiths are devastated. Ted is gone. A drunk driver. A hit and run. At least the police have caught the bastard, but there is no joy, no relief, no positivity, only emptiness.

3

The company that the Smiths use to organise Ted's funeral is called Hillier's Funeral Services. When they meet the owner, Tom, he's solemn and sombre. He speaks quietly and slowly, and is dressed in a dark, not-quite-black suit. Over the years he has learned to tone down his facial expressions and say very little and just nod a bit.

All of this is in total contrast to Tom's son, Mark, who also has a service-based business – one that arranges parties. Mark is regularly shit-faced on ecstasy and cocaine. He wears fluorescent Hawaiian shirts and has dyed his hair blue. Behind the scenes, Tom and Mark argue. Tom wanted Mark to join the funeral business, but 'No way' was Mark's perspective. However, Tom is now pleased that Mark didn't join, as he views his son's outlook very negatively and believes that had Mark joined the business, it might have been the death knell for it. Even so, Tom still worries that Mark being Mark and doing what he does is probably damaging Hillier's Funeral Services. Tom gets a lot of trade from strangers but less from the people who know him and his family, and the anonymous feedback he receives from his customers is glowing; therefore, he believes that having

Mark as a son must be bad for business.

The funeral is on a Wednesday. Derek hasn't worked in the previous twelve days, since Ted's death. Gertrude hasn't worked for years. She was an air hostess with British Airways until the twins arrived, and was going to go back and work for the airline company in a different capacity once the boys were born, as travelling around the world wasn't going to be possible now. But then all her mental health problems kicked in, so instead she concentrated on doing her best as a homemaker. She spent years zonked out of her mind on tranquillisers prescribed by her GP, but over the past ten years, since she was switched off the old tranquillisers and onto Prozac, she has been happier within herself and more communicative, though she's still quite flat and non-engaging in comparison to most other people. She's helped out with various charities since the boys reached sixteen, but since Ted's passing, she hasn't left the house; instead, she's been horizontal on the sofa in a self-made Bacardi haze – that is, until today.

Both parents are dressed in black, as is Mike, except he's wearing Ted's red cricket club tie. Ted was part of the club, though he didn't play cricket – neither he nor Mike were sporty – and it was Ted's favourite tie, so Mike is wearing it to feel close to him.

Tom Hillier has made sure that the casket containing Ted is at the church as planned. The family are traditional Church of England but never attend services, though Gertrude is known there as she helps out with fundraising fetes and other ventures. The vicar , John Jeffrey, already visited the house to pay his respects and to acknowledge the difficult time that Gertrude is going through. He knew Ted a little from the cricket club, but only to say hello.

Reverend Jeffrey gives the eulogy. Gertrude has a pounding headache, a Bacardi hangover. Mike is tearful, but Derek is holding it together by being like his grandad, even though he never met him, so he's really only going by what his own father, Robert, told him about him. Robert is present at the service. He is a resident in a care home now; he has mobility issues but is compos mentis. He has eighty per cent hearing loss and doesn't like wearing hearing aids. He can lip-read a little. His wife, Derek's mother, is deceased. Robert attracts a lot of stares at the service as he loudly questions the care home worker who is with him, asking for clarification on what exactly the vicar has said and what stage of the service they are now at.

Hillier's has provided four black limousines for the service as well as the hearse. Their employees bring Ted's casket to the hearse and drive all of the limousines. The Smiths sit in one by themselves. The vicar shares with Robert Smith and his carer, Derek's brother Todd, and his daughter Angelica. Todd is an accountant, unlike Derek. The privately schooled only child Angelica is reasonably good looking, but she thinks she's a supermodel, and even though she did okay with her A level grades and then at university, she incorrectly believes that she's a bit of an Einstein and has all the answers. Her contribution to the car conversation is, 'Ted should have been running on the opposite side of the road, facing the traffic; that way he would have been able to see the drunk driver, react and not get hit.'

Her father intervenes: 'Angelica, please, not now.'

Robert shouts at his son as he looks out the window, 'What, Todd, a cow?'

The carer doesn't know how to react, she doesn't

understand the family dynamics, but Robert is pleased when his son Todd responds, 'Yes, Father, a cow; lots of cows.'

The other limos contain some of Gertrude's first cousins; an ex-girlfriend of Ted's, Ellen, from years back when he was eighteen; and some of the Smiths' neighbours who don't have cars.

When they reach the crematorium, they have to wait; there is a schedule and a number of cremations are planned for the day. Once it's their turn, the vicar says some prayers, occasionally interrupted by Robert's loudness. Then the Elton John track 'I Guess That's Why They Call It the Blues' is played. It's one of Gertrude's favourites, and one she plays a lot in the house. Mike cries, Angelica advises that she's been to much better services, whilst Gertrude appears zonked and hums the Elton John song to herself. Derek tries to look composed and strong.

Todd says, 'Well, that's that.'

His father, Robert, responds, 'Yes, I agree, we should have worn hats.'

Todd nods and smiles.

Mike, meanwhile, looks over to his left in response to a voice he recognises, but there's no one there. Then he hears the voice again and sees what looks like an insect on the left shoulder of his overcoat. He hears the voice again and picks up the insect, but it isn't an insect. It looks like a very small version of his dead brother, Ted. Mike is a bit shocked and surprised. Somehow when Mike and Ted now communicate with each other, no one else sees or hears their interactions.

Ted says: 'Christ, it was hot in there. What a shit-show this is.'

There's a delay to Mike's response. 'That's what Angelica just said a moment ago.'

'First time I've ever agreed with that arrogant fuckwit on anything,' replies Ted. 'Let's get the fuck out of here.'

'You seem very different, Ted.'

An incredulous Ted raises his voice. 'No shit, Sherlock. I used to be a hundred and eighty-five centimetres tall and now I'm about one centimetre tall.'

Mike tries to explain himself better: 'No, that's not what I mean. The swearing, the anger, that's not like you. What's up?'

'What's up? What's up? Are you having a laugh? I was dead, but somehow I'm back, and unfortunately I'm the size of a small insect and am unable to communicate with anyone apart from you. There's a lot up, bro, I think.'

Mike pauses and considers this. 'Sorry, yes, you're right.' Then he follows up with, 'I like what you've done with your hair by the way, and where are your glasses?'

'That parting you have and I used to have, it was bloody awful. I'm wearing it brushed back from now on. And I don't need glasses anymore; I have perfect eyesight now, twenty-twenty in fact.'

'So, are you a reincarnation or what? And how come only I can see you?'

'I don't know, Mike, maybe it's a twin thing, maybe this happens with twins all the time. I really can't say; this is a first for me after all.' Then his mother catches his eye. 'Christ, Mum is so depressing. She keeps humming her favourite crap sad song.'

'She had it playing earlier when you were in the casket.'

'Fuck no, that's terrible. Come on, let's get out of here.'

'It's nearly over, but some people have been invited back

to the house. There'll be sandwiches and stuff to mark your passing.'

'Sandwiches to mark my passing and an Elton John song… this is fucking awful. Maybe I'd have been better off if I'd stayed in the burning casket.'

4

Once back at the house, Gertrude claims she has a headache. She makes herself a strong Bacardi and heads to the sitting room, which is just off the dining room, and lies on the sofa. Her cousins eye each other, a non-verbal communication thing, acknowledging the alcohol. They head over to Gertrude and what follows is quite unique: the two cousins talk to her while she hums the Elton John track and utters the odd word here and there, while the cousins engage with each other nonverbally via a code of various looks. This continues for some time in a cycle.

Derek has beef sandwiches because that's what his grandfather used to have, or so he was told. Angelica advises anyone who'll listen that she doesn't usually have sandwiches but will try a prawn sandwich; however, there aren't any, so she sighs. She doesn't want a tea or coffee, but will have some boiled water mixed with cold water, a slice of lemon and a cube of ice in a tall glass; it's good for detoxing, she says.

Ted is amazed that his ex-girlfriend Ellen is there. He tells Mike that she's not really an ex-girlfriend; he only ever went on three dates with her and it went no further because it looked like she would become an expensive girlfriend, as when they went out she would order lots of food. *Some things never change,* he thinks, as she has several half-sandwiches on her plate and has already demolished four others.

Uncle Todd steps away from his father, Robert, because Robert is now annoyed with him. Todd asked him if he wanted sandwiches on a plate, and Robert loudly berated him: 'Don't be stupid, son, of course I don't masturbate.'

For some reason at that moment the vicar went red in the face and avoided eye contact with the others. Robert's carer smiled.

Gertrude is feeling a little better; the Bacardi is doing the trick. She calls over to her husband for a refill, and he obliges, but she is less than impressed when she realises that what he has given her is iced water, so she makes her way into the kitchen and sorts herself out with another very large Bacardi.

Angelica passes Gertrude some ice as she prepares another of her own water concoctions and makes some small talk. 'I love your earrings, Aunt Gerty,' she says, which indeed is true; they're silver with a dark stone at the centre.

Gertrude smiles as she heads back to the sofa. 'Thank you. I'll leave them to you in my will.'

Angelica isn't sure how to interpret that as it was said without emotion. Was her aunt jesting? Was she being serious, or was she being a complete bitch like some of the girls used to be way back when Angelica was at her independent fee-paying secondary school? Angelica decides to just smile, and then she returns to the main room.

She approaches Mike. 'I'm so sorry for your loss.' Mike nods, gives her a peck on the cheek and says thank you.

Then she continues, 'I suppose the family should feel relieved that you were identical twins.'

'How do you mean?'

'Well, you were the same person, so in a way, we might not feel the loss. I suppose it's just you who will.'

Mike is stunned, but Ted is apoplectic. 'I knew she was a selfish airhead, but I never realised what a dickhead she was too. Then Ted combines the two words to create a new insult. 'She's a dair-head, a dair-head of the highest order.' Mike agrees.

Angelica sees some black olives on the table and puts her drink on the side so that she can put some into a small bowl for herself. Ted catapults himself down Mike's arm and leaps onto the table. He climbs onto a tall sauce bottle next to Angelica's drink. He unzips himself and pees into her water concoction. As he zips himself up, it's clear from Mike's facial expression that he's unimpressed. Ted just shrugs his shoulders. 'She was taking the piss. All I did was give her some more,' he says, and he cackles a laugh.

Mike says to his brother, 'Looks like Mum is taking this badly.'

Ted cackles again. 'Looks like she's taking it lying down to me.'

Mike puts on a stern face and says, 'Can you take this seriously, please?'

Ted blows a raspberry. 'It's my blasted wake, I'll do as I please, and it's totally shite too.'

'What did you want exactly, tinsel and a Mariachi band?'

'Actually, yes, something with a bit of verve and oomph.'

'Well, that's Dad for you; he's so traditional. You should have done a will.'

'Damn right I should have, and I should have stipulated

that Mark Hillier run the whole thing and not his boringly solemn father.'

Mike has a chortle. 'Could you imagine if we'd handed it over to him?'

'I heard a great story about the Hilliers. It was a few years back. The police were on to Mark; he was selling way too many drugs. Anyway, his grandmother had passed away and his dad, Tom, was overseeing the whole thing for his own mum. Mark decided to mark the occasion himself. Do a little something himself. While the body was in repose at the mortuary, he organised for a few friends and cousins to pay their respects. They were doing lines of Charlie on the casket. That was when the police raided.'

'Fuck no,' says Mike.

'Fuck yes,' says Ted. 'The joke around the place after and since is that when it comes to funerals, only Hillier's will do black and white. Tom was really pissed off.'

Mike smiles. 'That's hilarious. How come you never told me that before?'

'I just didn't. We were twins, Mike, but we weren't the most communicative of people. I don't think we ever got on, did we?'

'Maybe that was because we were too alike,' Mike responds. After a short pause he adds, 'We didn't not get on.' Then he moves the conversation forward: 'You don't appear introverted anymore; that's what I mean by you being different. And what did the police do to Mark?'

'I'm not sure, but it didn't end up in the papers and it never went to court.'

After about an hour, the vicar and Tom Hillier are the first to depart. Grandfather Robert and the carer are next. Then the only people Derek has been attending to, some of his work colleagues and some people he knows from the local Chamber of Commerce, head away. Next to go are Angelica and Uncle Todd, leaving Ellen as the last woman standing. Ellen hasn't said much all day but has at least paid her respects. Now she says, 'There's so much food left over. Shame if it goes to waste.' Mike smiles and offers her a doggie bag. As he shows her to the door, she peeks into the bag and squeals with delight when she sees the chocolate eclairs. 'Food heaven!' are her departing words.

'I think you had a lucky escape with her,' Mike offers to Ted.

'I bet she's got worms,' says Ted. Mike laughs. Ted continues, 'Could you imagine how unlucky you'd feel if she was living on your street and then there was an apocalypse and she was a zombie?'

'I know what she'd say to that.'

'Me too,' says Ted. 'Food heaven.'

They share a smile.

They walk back into the diner/sitting room area. Gertrude is asleep on the sofa. Their father repositions her so she's on her side. He does this a lot, to ensure that if she vomits, she won't choke. Then he sits at the table.

'Well done, Dad,' offers Mike.

'Thanks, Ted… sorry, I mean, Mike. A slip of the tongue,' says his dad.

'Old habits,' is Mike's reply, to which his father nods.

Ted interjects, 'Let's head to my room. This is starting to get depressing.'

Mike puts a hand on his father's shoulder. 'I'm going for a lie down.'

5

Mike sits on a chair in Ted's room. All of his stuff is still here. His brother had moved home six months earlier to try to save a deposit for an apartment.

Ted is scanning the room. 'Everything is so big,' he says. 'I'll never need a room this big again.' He pauses, then sighs. 'Dead at twenty-five. I never expected this.' Another pause. 'I never planned for this. I thought I'd live into my eighties.'

'I hear you.' Another pause. He continues, 'I wonder if this happens to us all?'

Ted gives him an angry stare. 'Everyone dies, you fool.'

'No, not that. I mean coming back as a miniature, like you have.'

Ted calms down and considers this. 'Who knows? Maybe.'

Another pause. Mike asks, 'Is there anything you regret, anything you wish you'd done while you were alive?'

More silence. Then Ted cries, 'Loads, to be honest, lots of things.'

'Life sucks sometimes.'

'It sure does,' Ted replies quietly.

Mike tells Ted he's tired and needs a nap and will head

into his own old room, which is now a spare bedroom. Ted understands, advising he'll chill where he is. Mike helps him onto the bed and onto a pile of his clothes that his mother has washed, dried, ironed and folded. Trousers, shirts, jumpers, boxer shorts and socks. Ted slips into a rolled-up pair of socks and thanks Mike, who heads away.

Ted finds it hard to settle; it's been a weird day. After a while, he exits the socks and travels around his room. He takes a look at his belongings. On the wall is the certificate for his degree in physics from the University of Reading along with some pictures: of his favourite sports team, the England cricket one; his favourite building, the Royal Opera House in Covent Garden; and the person he admired the most ever, Gandhi, so much so that his own glasses were shaped like the great man's. There are stacks of the journal *Physics Monthly* neatly placed in different parts of the room. Everything is neat, everything has a place, everything is organised. *My whole life amounted to this. Neat, tidy, meaningless, nothingness.*

After half an hour or so, he is genuinely tired and is ready for a kip. He's on the dresser and makes his way into the case that his glasses would usually be in and snuggles under the warm yellow cloth that he used to use to clean them.

Once Derek has done a small clean-up, putting a variety of things into the rubbish bin, the leftover food into green bags and the plates, bowls and cutlery into the dishwasher, he takes himself off to his room. He has a separate room to his wife. They haven't shared a bed for a decade. In fact, Gertrude, when drinking heavily, frequently doesn't make it as far as her room. The sofa is a regular resting place for her, but she has also been known to rest on the floor and in various other parts of the house.

Gertrude wakes to find drool hanging from the side of her face. She makes her way into the kitchen and uses a paper kitchen towel to wipe the self-made viscous fluid from her skin. She had forgotten about Ted's death, but then recalled it, and the pain has returned. She opens the cupboard and takes out the Bacardi bottle, unscrews the top and gulps it down for a few seconds. She uses the same paper towel to wipe the spirit from her jawline. Then she heads to the back door and out into the garden.

From the shed she pulls out the barbeque and wheels it into the centre of the garden. She takes some charcoal from a bag with her bare hands and puts it in place. Then she squirts some lighter fluid on the charcoal and sets it alight. She wipes her tears away, darkening her face with the charcoal dust from her hands, and then makes her way back into the house and returns with the clothes that were on Ted's bed and some of his *Physics Monthly* magazines. She places them on the flames and squirts more lighter fluid on top, and the fire takes hold with a whoosh.

A short while later, Mike rises from his slumber and slowly makes his way to the kitchen for a drink. Pouring himself a glass from the cold-water tap, he sees his mother in the garden and the flames on the barbeque. This, of course, is strange, but it's not unusual; not recently but in the past, his mother did many wacky things when under the influence. He peeps out the door. She's safe, so he'll just return to his slumber.

However, after he's taken one step away from the door, something internal encourages him to take a closer look, so he does. He is horrified. *That's some of Ted's things,* he thinks. *Christ!*

He runs down the hallway to Ted's room. The clothes on the bed are gone. Screaming and howling, he runs back up the hallway, into the kitchen and into the garden. He screeches at his mother, 'What have you done?' and kicks over the barbeque. What isn't already burnt falls onto the lawn, still burning but less so than when it was on the barbeque. Mike kicks out again, this time at some of the burning clothes, and stamps on those that he can, carefully avoiding the socks, as he doesn't want to squash his brother. Then he heads back into the kitchen and takes a small fire extinguisher from the sideboard next to the cooker. He returns to the garden and uses this to extinguish the flames.

Then his father rushes into the garden. Derek doesn't know what to think or do, but the adrenaline is flowing and his heart is beating fast.

Mike frantically searches through the now foamy and burnt clothes and the socks, before collapsing onto his back and crying out, 'You killed him! You burned him alive!'

Gertrude says nothing, but slowly returns to the house and makes her way down to her room. Derek doesn't know what to say or do, but after a minute he bends over, catching hold of Mike's hand. 'Son, let me help you up.'

They both re-enter the house, and while Derek closes the back door, Mike slowly and tearfully wanders back down to Ted's room. Derek doesn't follow after him; he considers it, but doesn't know what he would say once he reached him. He heads into the sitting room instead, and sits on the sofa that Gertrude was lying on earlier.

6

Mike kneels at the bedside, at the exact place the folded clothes were earlier. He cries into the duvet with his hands outstretched on the bed. Ted observes this from his place in the glasses case on the dresser. He's feeling a bit slow, as he only woke up a few moments earlier, disturbed by all the commotion in the garden, and now here's Mike, doing what he's doing.

Mike raises his face from the duvet and talks and cries at the place on the bed where the folded clothes previously were: 'I'm so sorry you're dead. I'm so sorry I couldn't save you from being burned to death by Mum.' Ted is alert now and finds all of this extremely odd. Then Mike looks up to the heavens; his face is red and his eyes are swollen. 'Ted, Ted, please forgive me.'

Ted is extremely confused, and in a very chilled-out, matter-of-fact way he says, 'Sure.'

Mike hears this and looks at the dresser to try to locate where the voice came from. He eventually sees Ted. He rushes to him and picks him up and hugs him close to his face. 'You're alive, you're alive!' Looking to the heavens, he says, 'Thank you, God.'

'I don't know what the hell is going on. I'm still dead, Mike, and if you don't take me off your face, there's a chance that as well as being dead, I'll drown too; those tears are huge.'

Mike puts Ted on the palm of his hand and bends down to talk to him. 'I know you're dead. What I mean is, I thought Mum had killed this new version of you by accident. That's why I was devastated – I thought I'd lost you for a second time.'

Ted doesn't understand but calmly says, 'Sure, whatever.'

'You know,' Mike says, getting excited now, 'I was thinking about what you said earlier. About never getting to do the things you wanted to do.'

'And?' queries Ted.

'Well, there are things I want to do. I suppose I now realise that I shouldn't put things off, because tomorrow isn't guaranteed.'

A pissed-off Ted replies, 'No shit.'

Mike sees his brother is annoyed and detects a certain change of tone. 'What's wrong?' he asks.

'What's wrong? What's wrong? I'll tell you what's wrong: I'm dead, me, that's right, me, I'm dead, and all I'm getting from you is tears and hardship, heavy, sad, emotional nonsense, and now this happiness and delight mumbo jumbo. You're so selfish. I'm the dead one here and all you can think about is you. Isn't it great that *you're* getting to benefit from my death, and that my death has given *you* life-changing realisations that mean you now get to focus on doing all the things in life that you could ever want to do? Where's your emotional intelligence, man? What about me?'

Mike is stunned by this monologue. He considers all this.

Then he says, 'I've never heard of emotional intelligence.'

'Exactly,' is Ted's response.

Before Ted can say anything else, Mike intervenes: 'I take your point, though. I'm lucky: I'm alive and I get to do whatever I want, and you don't. I'm sorry. I should have been less excited and more humble.'

Ted sighs. 'Don't worry about it. That's life, I guess.'

Then Mike, kind of thinking out loud, says, 'Maybe there's a way for you to do the things you always wanted to do, to actually do some of those things from your bucket list.'

'I don't see how. I'm a centimetre tall.'

'Stop being so negative.'

'I'm not, I'm being practical. It can't happen.'

Mike remains upbeat. 'What wouldn't you be able to do?'

Ted explains, 'I'm not going to be able to do Everest, am I? For starters, I wouldn't be able to get hold of an airline to take me to Nepal, but even if I could, I would struggle to pay for it. I can't even lift my passport now. And even if I could get there, climbing it, it would be a hundred and eighty-five times harder now, given my current size. It's impossible.'

Mike pauses for a minute, thinks about all of this, and then gently and calmly pushes back. 'Yes, you're right, you wouldn't be able to get there by yourself. But you could climb it by yourself if you got there, and yes, it would be a hundred and eighty-five times harder and take a hundred and eighty-five times longer, but you could do it, or I could climb it with you, so your size wouldn't be such an issue.'

'That's all very decent of you,' Ted says, 'but it proves my point. I can't do it; I'd have to rely on someone else.'

'Yes, but I'm happy to help out. We are brothers after all.'

'Yes, who never got on because we were so alike, and even though we're very different now, that doesn't automatically mean we're just going to start getting along with each other now.'

Mike doesn't give up: 'Yes, you're dead – it's a huge change; it can't ever be how it was for you. But you can still have a life, there are still things you can do. You're just going to have to adjust and adapt. And regarding us getting on or not getting on, well, I can't predict the future, no one can. So, do you want to do Everest or not?'

Ted thinks and says, 'No, I don't. That was just an example to prove a point.'

A moment passes. 'Oh,' says Mike, and then another moment passes. 'Fine,' he goes on. 'But if there are things you want to do, now is the time to say so, because I'm not wasting my time anymore. I'm getting on with writing my bucket list, and then I'm going to do those things that I want to do.'

7

Mike serves notice at the house in Reading that he's been sharing with three others. He's lived in that house since he graduated from university, the same uni as Ted, except Mike did a computing degree. Derek told them it was best that they go to Reading University so they could live at home, as it was a short commute; that way they wouldn't have to get loans for accommodation and would just have to get twenty-seven thousand pounds in loans for the fees only. These extraordinarily high fees were thanks to Cameron, Osborne and Clegg, known as The Three Tory Grifters of the Apocalypse by students everywhere. Though Clegg was technically in the Lib Dem party, many said he was really a Tory sleeper; after all, he had the background of, looked, sounded, and acted like a Tory. These high interest loans of up to fifty thousand pounds, mean many students end up being owned for most of their working lives by the people that own the banks, something many believe was purposely designed to keep those without money worried, poor and ill, and as a result make them submissive docile conformists to the plutocrats. University pals of Mike and Ted who found out the twins' rationale for choosing this university thought it was a great idea, and it led to them acquiring a nickname from fellow physics student Smart Alec: the Bracknell Bungalow Boys.

Gertrude just nods when Mike asks if he can move back in. His dad verbalises his assumption that it's for the same reason as Ted: to save up a lump sum for a deposit to buy a property. Mike doesn't correct him. He has savings, but has given up thinking about buying a property. He was saving, but house prices kept going up, which had a knock-on effect on the lump sum needed, and the increase in the deposit required was outstripping the amount he was able to save. It was like being on a ferry and despite moving forward and trying to reach the shore, he kept getting further and further away. He'd stopped saving up for a mortgage a year ago, and now with what's happened to Ted, he's decided that it's time to search for a greater purpose in life, as life is just too short.

He knows he doesn't want to be working in IT anymore, so he quits his job. Obviously, he doesn't tell his dad, just in case he won't let him move in. There's a chance that Derek would see the whole situation from his dead grandfather's perceived perspective, and God only knows what that would be. Why take the gamble that he might decide on a tough love approach and tell his son to stick with the job even though it bores him to death?

Ted doesn't care either way, but he does think Mike's ideas about jumping career are a bit far out and stupid. The first idea is to get a job in a geriatric hospital, but Ted manages to talk him out of that by saying, 'Imagine having to hang out with people like grandad Robert all the time.' The next idea is to get a job working for a homeless charity, but Ted is able to get Mike to dismiss that idea too by pointing out that they're hardly a good advert for the opposite of homelessness, given that as of right now they're both technically living at home aged twenty-five and are unemployed: the shame, the hypocrisy, the two-facedness.

Mike's third idea is to get a job in a children's home. Ted tries to talk this idea down too, but he has no success. Mike applies for some jobs in that field. He doesn't like misleading his father, but once he has a new job, he'll be able to explain that he's made a career change, which will be more easily heard. That's better than saying he quit his job without having another one lined up, which might freak Derek out.

8

On the day of the interview for a job as a support worker at the Better Futures Children's Home, Mike is nervous. He's wearing a suit. The children's home is in a deprived part of Reading and has been open for less than six months. It's part of a bigger organisation, the Better Futures Group. Mike is interviewed by someone from the head office of the group, but the manager of the home in Reading is present too.

The first question is easy to answer: 'Why do you want this particular job?' Of course Mike is able to give an excellent answer, about seeking a greater purpose after the death of his brother. Ted, who is present, thinks this is a load of tosh, and he fake-pukes in front of Mike and plays a fake violin, but Mike holds his nerve. He gets stuck, though, when they ask him about his experience of caring; he has no experience at all and isn't sure what to say.

Ted laughs at Mike's big pause and says to him, 'Your paws is so big, they'll think you're a grizzly bear.' Mike doesn't find this funny. Then Ted says mockingly, 'Well, way back you did care for Gregory, our pet goldfish.'

Quick as a flash, Mike blurts out, 'Way back I cared for

Gregory.'

An incredulous Ted is rolling around on the table, crying with laughter. 'You told them you cared for a goldfish! I've heard it all now.'

But Mike didn't mention the goldfish bit, and now he quickly adds that Gregory is his cousin, on his mother's side, who had ADHD when he was young, and that he, Mike, and his deceased brother, Ted, occasionally helped look after their cousin, to support their aunt, when they were teenagers.

The interviewers like the answer. Mike is relieved, and this answer has managed to end Ted's laughter, but now Ted is all serious, and whilst shaking his head, he says to his brother, 'Are you sure you're the right kind of person for this role? You just told a huge lie to try to get this job. If you look at the poster on the wall there, you'll see that one of their values is integrity. Are you sure you still have this? Well, do you?'

Mike, who has been finding it hard to ignore Ted's interference, just about does.

On the bus ride home, Mike tells Ted off, but he isn't having any of it; he has his fingers in his ears and shouts out 'La-la-la-la' whenever Mike tries to make a point. Once home, they see that their mum is lying on the sofa asleep. They can't tell if she's taking a nap or is in a stupor. Fifteen minutes later, Mike gets a phone call. The job is his. He's delighted, but Ted slates him.

'What do you know about kids? You can't even tie your laces,' he says. 'You know you'll be expected to cook some meals, from scratch. Not some pre-prepared stuff from Marks and Spencer that you can just bung in the microwave.'

Then Derek arrives home, and Mike excitedly tells his father, 'I've got a new job, as a support worker at a children's home.'

Derek doesn't have time to consider this, and automatically responds to the positive emotion; without thinking, he half smiles and says, 'Okay.'

The New Job

9

Mike is welcomed to Better Futures on his first day by the home manager, Melanie. Melanie originally started out working in admin for a local authority after she left school at sixteen. The first department she worked for was responsible for rubbish collection, then she was involved in car parks and parks. Then, to cover a maternity leave gap, she ended up working in children's services. She enjoyed that area the most, but when the administrator came back after giving birth to a son, Melanie ended up going back to car parks. Then a vacancy came up in children's services and she jumped at it. She worked in an admin role for four years and then took a job as a support worker in a children's home. She climbed to senior support worker roles, then got some project jobs, then became a deputy team leader, then a team leader, and after that she became a deputy house manager. She really loved that role; she probably loved that role the most, as she had lots of influence and authority, but the big positive was that she wasn't legally accountable for the home, as that's always the home manager's responsibility. Now in her fifties, she has been a home manager for over fifteen years. She takes it seriously, but being legally responsible for everything that happens as the home manager is serious and comes with a lot of pressure. She knows people get the sack from these jobs easily enough; if you don't manage your budget properly or if your face doesn't fit with the senior managers of the wider group, it's the door. But the real stress comes with legal accountability. She has seen how others have been blamed and taken to court over the years when things have gone wrong; it's a worry.

She makes Mike a coffee, and they sit together for fifteen minutes before Gemma, a project worker in her forties, starts Mike's induction.

Ted, who has been fake-yawning throughout Mike's conversations with Melanie, says, 'Thank God, I thought she'd never shut up. What a do-gooder.' But Mike is now chatting with Gemma and does his best to ignore Ted.

Gemma shows Mike into an empty bedroom. 'This is what the rooms look like. They're all en-suite, with a toilet and shower. The home has five rooms, and we currently have two that are empty. Having empty rooms is never good, as it makes balancing the budget harder. We did have four children here until recently, but one moved on last month. We're expecting two new kids this week, which means we'll be full for the first time.'

'Cool,' says Mike.

They pass the other empty room and then Gemma knocks on the door of an occupied bedroom. 'Are you dressed?' she asks. A female voice affirms that she is. Gemma opens the bedroom door and introduces Mike to a teenage girl, Bel. Mike exchanges pleasantries with Bel and then he and Gemma head back into the corridor, closing the door behind them.

Gemma whispers, 'Bel can be a bit mouthy, but she's fifteen, so it's to be expected, I suppose. She's been in a few homes. She was up in Rotherham for a while – you probably heard about that place, big scandal. She's had it tough in life.

'This next room belongs to Jez. He never knew his parents and was brought up by his aunt. But she died when he was thirteen and he fell in with the wrong crowd. He ended up in trouble and was convicted of a violent offence. He came here directly from the Feltham Young Offenders Institution. He was there for two years. He's sixteen now.'

Mike nods.

Gemma knocks on Jez's door. The response is an annoyed, loudish, 'What?'

Gemma calls, 'Jez, there's someone I want to introduce you to.'

'If it's that clown I saw coming into the house about thirty minutes ago, don't bother.'

'Don't be like that,' Gemma protests. She then whispers to Mike, 'He can be awkward and he's very territorial.'

Mike nods. Then he speaks up, addressing Jez: 'I just want to say hello.'

'Well, you've said it, so move on, tick your box.'

Gemma intervenes: 'Jez, please come to the door and say hello.'

They hear footsteps and then Jez opens his door. Pulling a face, he says in a sarcastic tone, 'Hello, nerd.' Then he closes the door.

Mike looks at Gemma and is a bit confused. Ted is

laughing at Mike. 'You muppet,' he says, the term he uses for his brother. Gemma shrugs her shoulders.

Mike calls out, 'Nice to meet you, Jez.' And then they move on.

They pass another room. Gemma beams a huge smile. 'This is Danni's room. She's an absolute star, and trust me, she's rare; I've never had one like her before and I've been doing this work for over twenty years. Her parents were druggies. Her dad went missing a long time ago and her mother's in prison, so Danni ended up in the system. You'll meet her later. She's out right now. We nickname her, behind her back of course, "The Jewel". She does all the right things, she's polite, she's ace at school. You know, she goes to a local grammar, which is rare for these types of kids let me tell you, and she also had the good sense to engage with therapy in the past when she needed it too.' Gemma gushes, 'She's my most favourite child ever.'

Mike nods. Gemma points towards a doorway. 'Let's head back downstairs and I'll introduce you to another project worker who's on shift here today.'

They head into the back yard and see a fit-looking male in his early twenties who's shooting a basketball at the hoop. He's both a decent dribbler and a good shot.

Gemma calls out, 'Gary, this is our new colleague, Mike.'

Gary shoots another hoop, catches the ball and puts it under his left arm. Approaching Mike, he extends his right hand and they shake. 'First day?' asks Gary even though he already knows the answer.

'Yes, it is.'

Gary passes him the ball. 'Go on, have a shot.'

Mike hesitates. Ted mockingly encourages him: 'Go on, Mike Jordan, you can do it.'

Mike decides to have a go; he's seen people do this on TV all the time. He doesn't bounce the ball, just carries it towards the hoop. He jumps and throws the ball; it hits the backboard and bounces away from the hoop.

'Hard luck,' calls out Gary and then follows up with a 'Whoops' as Mike lands awkwardly. Mike staggers, but just about manages not to fall over. Gemma smiles, and Gary says, 'Nearly there.'

Ted, meanwhile, is rolling around laughing his arse off as he mocks his twin. 'Always good to make a great first impression, Mike.'

10

Derek has chopped an onion and some green peppers and he adds them to the mincemeat he's been frying that's now brown. After a few minutes he adds in a tomato-based sauce from a jar. Mike has already set the table. No knifes, just a fork and a dinner spoon and a glass of water each for three people. Dinner chez Smith has been for three since Ted moved in a while back, and it's still for three now as Ted has been replaced by Mike. When setting the table, Mike didn't put himself where Ted used to sit; he set himself a place opposite to where Ted used to be. That was what he was going to do anyway, but he was also directed to do it that way by his dad, who said to not do so would upset his mother.

Derek lets the boiling water flow from the pot, and the strainer, behaving like Alcatraz, prevents the spaghetti from escaping. Then, using a particular claw-like utensil, he scoops the spaghetti onto three large plates. Mike helps out by shaping the spaghetti on the plate into a kind of circular inverted moat, a mound perhaps, and then Derek returns to the table with the pan and, using a different utensil, spoons bolognese sauce into the empty space inside the spaghetti mounds.

Mike leaves the kitchen and shouts out, 'Mum, it's ready.' He returns to the room and sits at the table saying, 'Thanks, Dad.'

Derek smiles and sits himself down and responds, 'Thank you, son.'

They don't tuck in; instead they wait for Gertrude. She arrives after about a minute, and she looks like she's been sleeping. She sits down and Derek stands up and helps push the chair in for her. 'Thank you,' she says.

Mike starts first. He uses the fork and spoon in a particular way, in tandem, spinning the fork, which somehow gathers the spaghetti around the fork, with the spoon playing a role to keep it in place. Then he puts the fork to his mouth and transfers much of the spaghetti on his fork into his mouth. Then, removing the fork and leaving the spaghetti behind, he is able to commence chewing. Any spaghetti outside his mouth is sucked in through his closed lips, which looks like the reverse action of a sausage maker.

Derek looks around the sides of his plate and then stands up and walks to a kitchen drawer. He returns with a table knife.

Mike says, 'Sorry, Dad,' to which his mum responds:

'Don't talk with your mouth full.'

Ted laughs, mocking his brother. 'Ha, she can't use that line on me anymore, sunshine.'

Derek smiles at his son and then starts to use his fork and knife to cut up all the spaghetti from its current eight- to ten-inch length to an average two-inch length. Then he puts down the knife and picks up the spoon, and uses the fork to push some of the spaghetti onto his spoon and then journeys it to his mouth.

Gertrude just has the fork; in a disinterested way she's using it to pick out bits of mince. It might be that she won't eat any of the spaghetti.

'How's the new job going?' Derek asks Mike.

'I didn't know you had a new job,' Gertrude says.

Not wanting to speak with his mouth full, Mike chews for what seems like an age. Ted just has to comment, 'Wow, my brother eats at snail speed.' Mike is listening but pretends to ignore him.

Once he has gulped down the last bit, Mike advises, 'I did tell you, Mum.'

'I must have been half asleep.'

'Drunk as an ass more likely,' is Ted's two pence worth. Mike agrees but says nothing, and if Derek could have heard what Ted said, he would have agreed too.

'So, the job?' Derek asks.

'So far so good,' Mike responds.

'What is the job?' Gertrude enquires.

'I've taken a job at a care home for children.'

Gertrude smiles, and Mike spins some more spaghetti.

Once his dad has swallowed his mouthful, he follows up with, 'Your great-grandfather would be very proud. He worked with children too.'

'Doing what?' asks Mike.

'He was a teacher.'

'Which great-grandfather?' Mike enquires.

'My dad's dad,' Derek replies.

Ted intervenes: 'You learn something new every day, don't you? Our great-grandfather, who we were told was a war hero, even though he never went to war, as he was an aeroplane grease monkey, was also a teacher.'

'I never knew that,' smiles Mike.

'I thought I'd told you,' Derek says. 'Yes, after the war, he trained as a teacher.'

Ted then pipes up, 'It's great that you've found this new job, Mike, but what about me?'

'What do you mean?' queries Mike.

'I have needs too.'

'You don't need a job because you don't need to earn a living.'

'Wow, you're so smart, Mike. Did you work all that out by yourself? Of course I don't need a job, but there are things I want to do. Otherwise what's the point in me being alive, or to be more accurate, in me being alive again.'

Mike, showing interest, asks, 'So, what's on your bucket list?'

'I want to rob a bank.'

Mike wasn't expecting this and as he's swallowing a mouthful some of it goes down the wrong way. He starts to choke a little and cough and goes red in the face. Derek gets up from his place and goes behind his son and slaps him on the back a few times. This has the desired effect, and as Mike wipes some of the tears from his cheeks, he thanks his dad for the intervention.

'Don't eat so fast,' is Gertrude's advice.

'If you end up dead, I'm not entirely sure what that will mean for me, brother dearest, so kindly chew your food properly,' is Ted's smirking contribution.

Mike is a bit pissed off. 'I nearly choked not because I was eating fast like Mum said or not chewing properly but because of the shock of what you said, Ted. Rob a bank… are you crazy?'

'No, of course I'm not crazy. It's just a bit like with you. You were looking for a deeper purpose and it looks like you've found it, but me, I need something too, a new experience, and it has to be one with a big buzz.'

'Yes, but a bank robbery? You just raised an important point, which is: what happens to you if I end up dead? Robbing a bank is dangerous. I could end up being shot.'

'This is England, Mike, not America; don't be stupid.'

Then Gertrude turns her face away from the table and vomits on the floor right next to where she is seated. 'I'm sorry,' she says and then starts to cry a little.

Derek calmly stands up. 'I'll clean that up, darling. I'm sorry, I mustn't have cooked it properly.'

Ted interjects, 'Yeah, Dad, you forgot to add the Bacardi.'

Mike gives Ted a look that says, *Don't be so insensitive.*

11

Melanie calls out 'Oi!' but Jez tries to pretend that he hasn't seen or heard her; he puts his head down and leaps up the stairs three at a time. Melanie heads into one of the day rooms and asks Neal, a man in his fifties who's a very experienced project worker, to join her upstairs.

'Jez has just come in. He has cuts to his face; it looks like he's been in a fight. I tried to talk with him, but he sprinted up to his room. Come with me, I can't confront him on my own.'

They head upstairs together and once outside Jez's door, Neal whispers to Melanie, 'The usual?' Melanie nods. Neal gently knocks on the door. 'Jez, can I come in, please?' There is no response. He tries again; no response.

Melanie winks at Neal. Then she opens the door and barges in. Jez wasn't expecting this so is caught off guard, and then he get his bearings and says, 'What are you doing?'

In a loud voice Melanie responds, 'No, what are you doing more like it? How dare you disrespect me like you just did.'

'I didn't see or hear you.'

'Sure. You blanked me and ran. Do you think I'm a fool?'

Neal gently interjects, 'Jez, your face is a bit cut up and grazed. Did someone hurt you?'

Jez tries to regain control. He steps away from them and says, 'Me? Me? Are you kidding, man? No one would mess with me.'

'Don't give me the tough man nonsense routine,' Melanie says.

Neal, still calm, says, 'Did someone do this to you, Jez?'

'No, man. Can I have some privacy now?'

Melanie shakes her head. 'I told you, Jez, I run a tight ship. If you've been fighting, I need to tell your parole officer. Is that what you want me to do?'

'No, Mel, no, everything's cool.'

'No, it's not cool,' she says and storms out.

Neal says, 'She gets upset because she cares about all of you and the house. So, what happened?'

'Nothing, man, I swear. I just fell.'

Neal doesn't say anything, he just slowly nods his head.

'Will she grass me up?'

'She should.'

'Shit, man. Neal, please have a word?'

'I'll talk with her, but you need to play the game, Jez, or you'll end up back in Feltham before you know it.'

'Okay, I hear you. Sweet.'

Neal heads off to speak with Melanie, feeling that their good cop, bad cop routine has yielded results of a kind. Jez takes off his top and steps into his en-suite. He turns on the cold tap and lets water fill his cupped hands before tossing the water up and onto his face. He does this a few times and is drying his face when Bel bursts into his bedroom. He turns as he hears her enter and steps out of his en-suite.

'What was that all about?' she enquires excitedly.

Jez continues to dry his face and then throws his towel to the side. 'Girl, you know boys and girls aren't allowed to mix in the bedrooms. Are you trying to cause me grief?'

'Sounds like you can do that all by yourself, and anyway, is a tough man like you really worried about Melanie and Neal? Come on, Jez, Neal is wet.'

'I gotta play the game.'

'So, what happened to your face?'

Jez swaggers around his room with his top off and lies to her: 'Some guy took issue with his woman being more interested in me than him, so I had to teach him.'

'Looks like it was you that got teached.'

'Nah, no chance, I take no shit in my manor,' he says and flexes his muscles.

'Nice six-pack,' Bel compliments.

'So are you going to be my girl?'

'Only a minute ago you were worried about me being in your room and now you want me to be your girl?'

'Don't worry about the confusion. So are you my girl?'

Bel laughs, but not loudly, then says, 'Show me the money.'

Jez points to his dresser where there are lots of coins: pounds, fifty-pence pieces and twenty-pence pieces. Bel laughs again; they are clearly on the same page humour-wise. 'Not enough,' she says.

She turns away and heads from the room, and then from the doorway looks back at the grinning Jez and, just before she steps out of his eye line, says, 'All my exes had cars.'

12

'C'mon, brother, say yes.'

Mike isn't pleased. 'No, robbing a bank is a stupid idea.'

'There's nothing stupid about doing robberies,' is Ted's response.

'Robberies, you want to do robberies? You see, there's the problem right there: you haven't even done one, and you've already decided you want to do loads. Bank robbers get caught because they don't quit while they're ahead, and we've never been in trouble, so we're well ahead right now and therefore we should quit this stupid idea right here.'

'No, I just want to do one; it was just a figure of speech, the loads bit.'

'We know nothing about robberies.'

'It's not that hard. You walk into a bank, threaten the teller, get the money, walk out, drive off,' Ted calmly explains.

'Problem number one: I don't know how to drive.'

'No sweat, I'll teach you.'

'Problem number two: I have never threatened anyone in my life.'

'No time like the present to learn a new skill.'

'Ted, this is crazy.'

Ted doesn't respond. He goes quiet.

After a minute, Mike re-engages. 'Sorry, but I can't help you with this. It just isn't me.'

'Neither was childcare, but now you're working in a children's home.'

'That's not comparable at all. Working in the home is about doing good. Robbing banks is the opposite of that.'

'It doesn't have to be. I don't need the money, I can't spend it; I just want the buzz.' Mike has his arms folded. Ted continues, 'Banks are no one's friend; they're out for themselves and the rich. Look, we couldn't even get mortgages.'

'Robbing one would still be a bad thing.'

'No, it wouldn't, not if we gave the money to charity, a children's charity even,' is Ted's manipulative line.

'So I'm supposed to be Robin Hood now, and you, I suppose, you want to be Little Ted.'

'Hey, less of the little jibes, please. I'm pretty sensitive about that for obvious reasons.'

'It's wrong,' argues Mike.

'It was wrong lying on your CV and then at the interview to get a job in a children's home.'

'There's a big difference between those things and this.'

'No, there isn't. You are just being selfish now. You're happy to break the law for yourself, but not for me.'

'It doesn't feel like a good idea.'

'I hear you,' says Ted. Then he calmly adds, 'Okay, let's just have a look at a bank. We can walk around one, and then we can see how you feel after that. We'll just have a look, okay?'

Mike is still touchy. 'What you mean is we'll case a joint?'

'Not exactly, but kind of. It isn't against the law, you

know, to look a bank over.' Mike is thinking. In an even more chilled-out tone, Ted says, 'C'mon, brother, let's just have a little look, and if after that you don't feel comfy, fine, we won't do it.'

'We'll just look?'

'We'll just look.'

'Swear to it.'

Ted laughs. 'Of course I swear – cross my heart and hope to die, stick a needle in my eye.'

13

Alf arrives at the children's home; he's fifteen and from Ealing. He has always been the weakest puppy in the litter, always picked on, always beaten up, and even though he has grown physically strong, he is so psychologically beaten down that he has zero confidence and an inability to defend himself verbally. He has a slight learning difficulty too, which hasn't helped. He has been in care for years, a child of neglect due to his parents' inability and disinterest in caring for him. For some reason he is a big fan of all things Japanese – the culture, that is.

Gemma shows him around the home. He likes his room; everything is newer than in his last place. As she is showing him about, they encounter Gary, who is exercising. Gary talks to Alf whilst continuing to exercise and convinces Alf to join in the exercise session, and they start doing star jumps together.

Jez happens to wander by and starts to mock Alf even though they have never met. Jez has been expecting a new kid and reckons this must be him. He doesn't need an introduction to Alf before he starts imposing himself. He wants to make sure that the new boy immediately understands the hierarchy.

Alf doesn't engage, he puts his head down, but Gary intervenes and, appropriately, tells Jez off. Jez responds as he leaves the area by mocking the unbranded trainers that Gary is wearing. Danni witnesses this from her window.

14

Melanie is über excited and shows the new girl, Jane, around herself. This will be the first time that the home has been full. Jane doesn't say much. She nods her head to highlight she understands everything and smiles when introduced to people, but she says very little. This is her third home. She's a Hackney girl. Her first children's home was in Essex, but she kept running back to Hackney, so for her own benefit, she was moved further away from London, and she ended up in Lancashire. She looks sad and she is, but she's also very pleased to be back in the south.

At five p.m. all five children meet for the first time in the dining room for supper. Melanie ensures she is present to mark the occasion of having five in the house. It's homemade pizzas and salad all round. Initially, Danni is the only child who eats the salad, but with some positive encouragement from Gary, Alf starts to eat his too. Jane speaks for the first time, advising that she will try the salad if Melanie promises to take her on a trip to London. Melanie encourages her to eat the salad but doesn't make any promises.

Bel says, 'Jane, you and me will be going to the same local comprehensive. If you don't want to eat your greens there, you don't have to.'

Alf asks Gary, 'Will that be my school too?'

Gary doesn't know the answer, but Melanie advises, 'No, love, you're going to a different place that will meet your exact needs.'

Jez sniggers and adds, 'Yeah, you're going to a special school for slow people, dumbo.'

Danni says, 'Alf, I heard the school you're going to is really good, so take no notice of Jez.'

Alf smiles. Melanie says, 'Jez, please.'

Gary bites back on Alf's behalf: 'You're one to talk, Jez. You aren't even allowed to go to a comprehensive; they keep you isolated and out of general circulation.'

An excited Bel cheers. 'Jez is so cool, he goes to a PRU.' They all know this means Pupil Referral Unit.

Then Melanie follows up with, 'You're all mostly going to different types of schools, but they fit your unique needs. Anyway, can we please concentrate on the food now?

15

Sometimes Jez heads to bed early and once the house is quiet he sneaks out the window. It's a short drop onto a flat roof – he does it gently so as to make as little noise as possible – and then from the flat roof it's only one storey to the garden. He creeps about and it isn't until he is about fifty metres from the home that he straightens up and starts his swagger.

Tonight, Jez queues to get into Gringos nightclub. He behaves whilst in the line, but once he gets to the door the bouncers block his entry; they say nothing to him, just shake their heads and point him away.

He says, 'C'mon, man, I'm nineteen.' Again the bouncers say nothing, just smile and look over him. He knows he won't be getting in, so he slinks away.

A couple of streets away is Bright nightclub. He queues and again behaves himself; he wants to get in. But at the door the bouncer says, 'Sorry, son, you're too young.' Jez doesn't argue the toss and again moves on.

There is another nightclub a street away, Knights. He decides to change tactics. Standing alone, he thinks, hasn't helped, and as a result he's been attracting the wrong kind of attention from the doormen, so this time he stands next to a group of four females, aged about nineteen and twenty. He starts talking to them, and they are enjoying his chat. He knows he will get in. But then, as the five of them are nearly at the front of the queue, two blokes in their twenties approach Jez and one of them pushes him in the chest and angrily asks him, 'What the fuck do you think you're doing with my girlfriend?' Verbals are exchanged, and the bouncers, who know the aggrieved boyfriend, back him, and while he gains entry, Jez is told to get lost.

He walks around town for another thirty minutes or so, and then he heads home. Once he is about fifty metres from the home, he loses the swagger and creeps into the back garden. He places a garden chair against the wall of the house and climbs up onto the flat roof. From the flat roof he is able to extend his arms upwards and, with a small jump, grab hold of the window ledge. Using his feet, he scrambles his way up the wall and climbs back into his room. Then he kicks off his trainers and lies on the bed.

16

'We should really try and do something nice for Mum,' says Mike.

'What, like buy her flowers and stuff?' asks Ted.

'No, something real big that would cheer her up.'

'We could give her a few grand if you like.'

'No, she'd only drink it,' is Mike's response. Ted nods in agreement. Then Mike pipes up, 'I was thinking more like, maybe go meet Elton John or something and get her his autograph.'

'Really?'

'Yes, really.'

'Um, well, fine. Do you know where he lives? We'll just go round.'

17

Bel hasn't really gelled with Danni, they just haven't clicked, but there's no animosity. Jane seems like she's really far away and is quite distracted. Bel likes Jez, he's kind of cool, but he tends to do his own thing, and Alf isn't the kind of person Bel wants to be associated with, so this afternoon she heads out on her own.

She ends up in the local park. She has a walk about. There's a group of boys playing football, some wearing the shirts of famous clubs. There are some families sitting on blankets. *Those children look so happy,* she thinks to herself, and then she composes herself, hardens herself – she doesn't want to go there, she doesn't want to feel vulnerable, she doesn't want to admit to herself that she feels she is lower than nothing.

There are two areas in the park with swings and obstacles in them for kids. There's the side that's clearly for toddlers and under-fours, and there are a few youngsters being supervised there. One woman, Laura Giggs, catches Bel's attention because she loses her temper and shouts at her children, three-year-old Massie and six-year-old Donna, for not trying and making more of an effort to play. Then there is the side that's for older children, probably under-twelves, and there's no one there. Bel heads into this side and walks towards the swings, and just chills out there, sitting on a swing.

This lasts a few minutes until a group of teenage girls approach. Bel doesn't know what to expect from them, but strikes a positive note by saying hello. One of them responds by also saying hello, but unfortunately she does so in a mocking way, slowly, whilst making a face and walking hunched up. The other girls laugh.

Then another says, 'Look at the size of the spot on her face,' and they laugh some more.

'Girls, that's what happens when you don't wash,' says another girl, and then turning her attention to Bel, she snarls, 'you filthy bitch.' They all laugh.

A different girl calls Bel a fat slob, and even though she knows she isn't, as she's only a size eight at best, it makes her feel self-conscious and it hurts. Bel decides not to respond. The abuse continues for a few minutes and then they all move on.

Not long after this a bloke in his late twenties appears; Johnson is his name. 'Don't mind them, they're young and stupid, probably only fourteen or fifteen, and obviously jealous of you.' Bel smiles. Johnson adds, 'It's probably because you look good and are obviously much older than them.'

Bel smiles again, and this time she adds, 'Thanks.'

Johnson sits on the swing next to her. 'You must be about eighteen?'

She composes herself and, plucking up some false courage, lies, clarifying that she is indeed eighteen.

'Here, have a ciggie,' he says.

18

Jane is missing. The staff have checked every room in the house, the garden and the outside buildings. Mike heads off for a walk around the local area with Ted, to see if they can find her. Gemma has taken out the car and is driving around the shopping and nightlife areas that are about a mile from the house. They scour this part of the town. Nothing. The staff are worried. Gemma and Melanie are both experienced and know this type of thing happens, but they also know it isn't a good look for the home and that the regulator and social workers will look at the house more closely because of this. Gary is nonplussed and does some chin-ups and sit-ups with Alf, who hasn't quite grasped that Jane is missing.

Mike is quite concerned. 'She's only fifteen,' he reminds Ted.

Ted doesn't know what to think, as he is more focused on figuring out what he wants to do with his new life. He just shrugs his shoulders and nods to acknowledge his brother's anxiety. Jez thinks it's cool, but Danni is concerned. However, it's Bel's perspective that's most revealing: 'Even if she turns up murdered, who would care? We're the invisibles – no one gives a shit about us.'

The other children say nothing, but Melanie intervenes with an appropriate, 'We care about you all.' None of the children respond to this, though; it looks like they don't quite believe Melanie's line.

The police come round and take details, but there are zero sightings of Jane for a whole two days. Then there's a knock at the door. It's the British Transport Police; Jane was picked up by them after she was detained for being on a train without a ticket. She refused to speak with the police, she said absolutely nothing to them, but soon enough they cross-matched her on the system and recognised that she was the missing kid.

Gemma tries to hug Jane, well, she does hug her, but Jane just stands there, unresponsive. Gary, who was passing, takes the report from the policemen and then notices the biceps on one of them and asks a fitness question about weights and repetitions. The police head away and Jane is followed into her room by Gemma. Gemma asks her if she is okay, and Jane nods. She sits on the bed and Gemma sits nearby on a chair.

'Where were you?' Gemma asks.

'I don't want to talk,' is Jane's reply.

Gemma senses that the best thing to do right now is not to push it, as she hardly knows Jane. 'Okay, we can pick this up later. All that matters is that you're here now, and are safe.'

19

Ted sings a Roy Orbison classic to Mike, '*Crying*'. Mike isn't amused and tilts his head to the side to try to wipe some of the tears off his cheek and onto the short sleeve of his T-shirt. He just about manages to do so, and is chided by Gemma, who walks into the kitchen and warns him about not concentrating while he is using a sharp knife. Then she advises him that if he were to wear the kitchen goggles/glasses, then the vapour from the onions wouldn't reach his eyes and there wouldn't be any tears.

'Next time I'll use them, next time,' he responds.

Ted says, 'It's a bad state of affairs when your brother cries more whilst cooking than he did at his own brother's funeral.'

'That's not the case. I was upset and I did cry.'

Ted recognises this but decides to wind his brother up a little bit more. 'Sure, tell yourself whatever it is you need to, to feel less guilty.' There's a pause and then he follows up with, 'I still want to rob a bank, you know.'

'Here we go, still going on about robbing banks. It's not a good idea, Ted.'

'So what? Good idea, bad idea, I don't care. I'm just

saying, it's still on my mind, it's still on my list of things that I want to do before I die.'

Mike tips the onions into a bowl of mincemeat and flour and mushes it all together. Homemade burgers are on the menu tonight. 'Things to do before you die, sure. Thing is, robbing a bank, if it goes wrong… Do you see the mush I'm making here? This is what we'll end up looking like.'

'God, you're so dramatic.'

An hour later burgers, peas and oven-cooked chips are served up. Alf loves the burger but isn't a fan of onions, so picks through the burger and removes the onions as he sees them, or if he encounters them in his mouth, he uses his fingers to put them onto the side of his plate. Danni uses her dessert spoon to eat her peas, while Bel struggles to corral her peas onto the fork. Jane doesn't touch her food despite the encouragement to do so.

Jez has tucked into the chips and has half the burger eaten when he smiles at Bel. 'You're funny the way you suck up the peas.'

Bel replies, 'I'm good at sucking things,' and smiles back at him.

Ted says to Mike, 'You can't let that go, you have to intervene.'

Mike hesitates, but recognises he's right and says, 'Bel, please, it's not appropriate to say things like that.'

She doesn't react, but Jez does. He takes another bite of the burger and then spits it onto his plate and puts his finger into his mouth to scrape more of it out. 'This burger is shit, man. I've seen better come out of a dog.'

Alf laughs. Danni reassures Mike that the food is good. Mike isn't sure what to say. Jez stares at him, then pushes his plate into the centre of the table, stands up and leaves the room.

Ted says, ‘Why do you want to do childcare, Mike? It’s tough work, and you’re crap at it too.’

20

Alf is getting quite fit. There is something about Gary that makes him feel good about himself. Alf has had people be nice to him in the past; he thinks they were probably nice enough people, but they were also getting paid. With Gary, though, it feels like he is actually very interested in helping Alf.

Gary has different tasks to do around the house, but the only thing that he is ever really interested in is the exercise, so much so that he thinks that someday he will open his own gym. The kids aren't usually interested in working out, so he feels underused, but Alf is impressionable, and has decent muscle mass and coordination, so Gary is extra motivated to help him in a way that he hasn't been with the other kids. He feels like he can actually achieve something with Alf. The boy is a bit slow, but Gary has learnt that as long as he shows him how to do things in stages, he generally does pick them up.

21

Laura Giggs drops in to see her GP. Dr Irene Nolan knows her quite well. Laura has been sectioned in the past and it was Dr Nolan who had to assess her and sign one of the forms to have her hospitalised against her will. Laura has bipolar disorder, and it was the mania presentation that led to the sectioning. They were worried about her; she had become a bit paranoid too, and wasn't eating or drinking. Her state also increased their concern for the welfare of Laura's two young children. Massie didn't realise anything was wrong at the time, she was so young, but Donna, being older, did feel the impact of being taken from her mother and placed with foster parents. Thankfully, six months later, once Laura had been back home for two months and was recovering well, the children were returned to her.

Laura visits her GP quite often, but it is never to do with her, it is always with concerns of one kind or another regarding her children: they are ill or sick or something isn't quite right. Dr Nolan always gives them a check-over and generally believes them to be in good health, though sometimes they do appear undernourished.

Dr Nolan sees the three of them today, and Laura is

complaining that the children are lethargic. While she is physically examining the girls, Dr Nolan discreetly assesses Laura's mental state. The children do appear a bit lethargic, but by and large, apart from some occasional diarrhoea and appearing a little underweight, they are okay. The doctor does wonder about Laura, though. Laura seems a bit stressed, but of course being a mum and worrying about the children might explain this. Laura isn't reassured about her children's health, but she thanks the doctor nonetheless and leaves.

One of the medical practice receptionists rushes in to see Dr Nolan before the next patient is presented. 'Doctor, that last lady, Laura Giggs, I saw her in the park a few days ago with her children. She was shouting at them and scolding them.'

'Did she strike them or anything?' asks the doctor.

'No.'

'Did the children look scared?' asks the doctor.

'No, they didn't.'

'Okay, thanks.' Dr Nolan considers this for a moment. Then she reopens Laura's file and searches for the email address of Laura's community mental health nurse.

22

Mike can't drive, so a taxi will be required to get to Elton's place. Obviously, a taxi door to door would cost too much, so the plan is to get a bus, a train and then a taxi; that works out much better financially. They know Elton's address from the internet, so they make the journey and get dropped off there by a taxi. Mike presses the bell on the intercom. After a while, someone answers.

Mike says, 'Hello, my name is Mike Smith. I would like to speak with Sir Elton John, please.'

The man at the other end says, 'Speaking.'

An excited Mike says, 'Really? Is that really you, Elton?'

A bored and clearly frustrated Elton says, 'Yes.'

Then, excitedly, Mike says, 'Great. I need a favour.'

But before he can say anything more, Elton responds, 'I don't think so. Fuck off.'

Mike is surprised. Ted just shrugs his shoulders. They call a taxi and use the same routes and methods to get home.

23

Jane is heading out for a stroll to the local park. Alf asks if he can join her, and she shrugs her shoulders to indicate, *Sure, why not*, but Alf doesn't read the signal. He turns away and she recognises that he hasn't understood her, so she calls out to him, 'Yes, you can.' He turns to her with a smile that he usually reserves for Santa Claus.

They walk around the streets for a while before they head into the park. They spend time sitting on the swings and have a good laugh on the roundabout. Jane holds on tight as Alf uses all his might to get the wheel spinning very fast, before he jumps on himself. As it starts to slow, he jumps off again and, using his strong arms and body, builds up the speed again, before jumping back on. He does this several times. It's a big buzz for the pair of them.

That night Jez sneaks out again, onto the flat roof and then quietly out onto the street. He is looking for action of some kind, a buzz, anything to make him feel like a somebody; he needs some self-worth, some validation. He heads back to Gringos nightclub and again they say nothing and just wave him away. He heads to Bright nightclub and they say, 'Come back in two years, son.'

He heads to a place he hasn't tried before, Places nightclub, and starts chatting to some females in the queue, but one of the males with them tells him to 'Fuck off,' so he does.

He walks up to Knights nightclub and one of the door staff smiles. 'I remember you. No chance.'

Jez walks away and stands at the corner, trying to decide what to do next. Then he hears a voice: 'I can get you into nightclubs.' It's a man in his thirties, dressed in cool and clearly expensive branded clothes.

Jez says, 'I have ID, man. I'm eighteen.'

The man takes the ID and looks at it and laughs. 'I had one of these when I was thirteen.' Then the man asks, 'What's your real age, Jez?'

Jez tells him the truth.

'Sixteen, that's a good age,' says the man. 'I'll get you in here. I've been looking for someone like you. You'll have to scratch my back, though, but there'll be some pocket money in it for you.'

They shake hands. The doorman sees that Jez has been talking with Kenny. Jez approaches the Knights nightclub doorway again. Kenny nods at the doorman and the doorman lets Jez pass and also tells the cashier not to charge this Jez the admission fee. Jez is doubly delighted.

24

Neal has worked as a project worker for about ten years now. Out of all the people at the home, it's Neal that Mike feels he has something in common with. Neal had worked in marketing, but when his brother died from a drug overdose, it had a major impact on him. He felt guilty about not being more present and helpful, and his brother's death was the lightbulb moment that took him away from marketing and into care, initially as a drug worker and then into working with children in care. He believes there are strong links between the two lines of work, as many of the children he has worked with ended up in care because of the chaos that surrounded their parents, who struggled with drugs, mostly heroin and other opioids. He is always talking to the children about the danger of drugs and the importance of staying clear and clean.

He is out and about today with Alf. 'A gentle soul' is how Neal would describe Alf. They are strolling about the shopping centre and other shopping areas, just having a chill. Neal is assessing how good Alf is with managing his pocket money. It turns out he's not good at all, as he has given it all to Bel already. Neal agrees to buy him a treat and Alf chooses a large moon-shaped lollipop. On the walk back he decides not to untie the ribbon to take off the see-through plastic wrapper. 'I'm saving it,' he says.

When he gets back to the home, he hands it over to Bel, and then Alf explains to Neal, 'I was saving it for Bel.'

She squeals with delight. 'I do love a gift, but when I said I'd lick your lollipop for you, this isn't what I meant.'

Jez gets angry when he sees and hears this interaction, and he picks up a chair and smashes it against the wall. Bel isn't startled at all; in fact, she finds it exciting.

Ted comments to Mike, 'Alf is such a dumb-ass,' and starts to make donkey noises, which gets a smile out of Mike.

Neal relaxes when he sees that Jez is just walking away from the area and doesn't intend to pick up the broken parts of the chair to use as a weapon, which is something he has seen happen elsewhere in the past.

Melanie is quite worried about the dynamics. She takes Bel into a quiet room and sits with her. 'Bel, love, what happened between you and Alf?'

'Nothing, he just likes me.'

'Of course, you're very likeable, but what you just said to him, what was that all about?'

'That's private.'

'Given that you said it publicly, I'd say it isn't private at all.'

'I don't see what the big issue is,' snaps Bel.

'The big issue is that Alf is a vulnerable child.'

'I'm a vulnerable child.'

'Indeed you are, but in a different way to Alf. The language you used was quite sexual; is there something going on between you?'

'No, I was only joking with him because he gave me money.'

'Did you promise him something in return?'

'I said words, but I didn't mean them. Come on, Melanie, Alf didn't even know what I meant.'

'So were you mocking him?'

'No, not mocking, just playing.'

'And why was Jez so worked up? Have you said anything similar to him?'

Bel laughs. 'It looks like Jez is the jealous type.'

'Have you made him any promises similar to the one you made Alf?'

'I was joking with him too.'

'Bel, you need to be careful with your words and the impression that your words can give to others.'

'I have had sex, you know; I'm not a child.'

'I know you've had sex, Bel, but you are a child.'

'I'm fifteen, I'm not a child, and you can't stop me from having sex.'

'That's not what I'm saying, Bel.'

'Yes, it is, you old cow. You're just jealous that men are interested in me and not you.'

Melanie lets out a small sigh. 'Our conversation is moving in the wrong direction, Bel. Let's end it now, but we'll come back to this later.'

Bel stands up and walks out of the room without saying anything more. Melanie thinks to herself, *It's good to have all the beds full, but caring for children is complex and demanding.*

25

Gemma is Mike's supervisor. They meet regularly and she is showing him the ropes.

'Continuity is an important building block for children and that's one of the reasons why children's services try not to remove children from their parents, but sometimes it's inevitable.'

Ted interjects, 'Tell her we've seen the movie *Annie*,' and then he starts to perform 'It's A Hard Knock Life'. Mike doesn't let on that he's enjoying Ted's performance and looks at Gemma directly and nods to show he's listening to her.

'Despite the importance of continuity, a number of children frequently move between different foster parents and different children's homes too. Where Danni has been lucky is that she has always been academically bright, and for her, the continuity has been in her schoolwork: her subjects have been the same, and she likes them, and finds them easy and interesting. Next year she'll do her GCSEs, and she expects to get at least an A in eight of her subjects and Bs in the other two. She isn't sure what subjects she'll do for A level. I think she'll do physics, chemistry, biology and maths, but Melanie thinks she might end up doing economics.'

26

Bel and Jane go to the same school but aren't in the same class, and today when they arrive at the school gate, Jane keeps walking past the school and, without looking at Bel, just says, 'Laters.' Bel thinks nothing of it; she pauses for no more than a second and then just walks through the school yard and heads into the school building.

Jane waits in the corner of the park and when her accomplice arrives, they change out of their school clothes and into their normal wear. They put their uniforms into their school bags and hide the bags in a ditch. Then they head off to the train station.

Alf is very excited. 'I feel like Ferris Bueller.'

This gets a smile from Jane, though she hasn't seen the movie that Gary and Alf watched on Netflix. She says, 'It won't be an adventure at all if we can't get through the barriers and onto a train.'

Once they're at the station, she explains what they need to do, and then she expertly shows him, by closely following a woman who has legally activated and opened the barrier by swiping her travel pass. 'Timing is everything. The barrier doesn't stay open for long and if you dillydally for even a second, it'll touch you as it closes. That won't hurt or even block you from getting through, but it will sound an alarm. It goes off for three seconds, which attracts attention and can alert the staff to the possibility of wrongdoing.'

Alf has never run this gauntlet before; it's exciting, and he doesn't want to get caught – he wants to get through undetected, or the adventure will be over before it has even started. He makes it through before the barrier closes, but in doing so, pushes into the back of the man who is going through. The man is about to mouth off, but when he looks at Alf, he understands what Alf is trying to achieve. The man looks over at the station worker who is manning all the gates and sees that he has been distracted by having to assist someone with fishing out a stuck ticket. He smiles at Alf and steps aside, giving way, and simply says, 'After you, young man.'

Alf is buzzing – what a coup! He is through undetected and the businessman with the umbrella was nice to him as well. He catches up to Jane and they wait for the train, and once they're on it, they remain standing.

When the schools notify the children's home of the non-attendees, Neal heads down to the train station on the off chance that Jane and Alf might be there, but they are long gone. In fact, they are about to pull into Paddington in London. They seem to gel together as a duo quite well; it's chilled out between them and there is no need to impress each other. Jane explains the next part of the adventure to Alf: getting through the barriers again, then a walk to an overground train station and onwards to Hackney Central. Jane can see that Alf is harmless and feels some pity for him as others mock him without him realising it. Alf likes that she is nice to him, warm and kind.

They make it to Hackney Central, and from here it's a ten-minute walk until they arrive at some council flats. To get to the different levels, you have to get through a locked communal door. Jane buzzes a random flat, and when a voice answers, she tries to deepen her voice a little and says, 'It's the postwoman.' She is buzzed through.

Jane leads the way up four flights of stairs and they step onto what looks like a long outdoor balcony. It has over a dozen individual front doors, some to council properties and others to properties that are ex-council, now privately owned through the Right to Buy scheme. Jane heads to number 320 and reaches under a plant pot and finds a key. Using it, she opens the front door. She sits Alf in the lounge and heads up the stairs into the bedroom part of the maisonette.

A woman calls out weakly, 'Who's there?'

Jane replies, 'It's me, Mum, Jane.'

Once in the bedroom, Jane kicks off her shoes and lies next to her mother in the bed.

'You kept your word, sweetheart. You said you'd come again and you have.' Her mum slowly wheezes this out through her face mask and past the sound of the flowing oxygen.

They lie there for an age.

27

At the end of the school day, Bel is picked up by a man in a car. It's Johnson. He's the man who gave her the ciggies in the park. They have been meeting up regularly. He buys her gifts, things like cigarettes, cheap perfume, makeup, sweets and ice cream. On the fourth meeting he gave her a box of condoms and eleven of these have since been used, so he will need to buy her another twelve pack. Once they have spent some time together at his place, he drives her back close to the children's home.

'I love you,' he says.

Her heart is racing. 'I love you too. You're the most amazing person I've ever met,' she admits.

28

Alf has been very bored but has said nothing. On the way to Hackney, Jane explained that her mother is dying and that she wants to spend some time with her. He's cool with that and just watches TV.

At around seven p.m. Jane tells her mum that she has to go but that she'll return again. They both cry and then Jane heads downstairs. She and Alf exit the maisonette and walk down the covered stairwell. They close the self-locking communal front door behind them. It's then that Jane freezes in shock. She is face to face with a man in his sixties.

'Hello, Jane,' he says. He steps towards her, hugs her and tucks some of her hair behind her ear. 'What an unexpected surprise. Visiting your mum, I presume?'

'Yes,' is the robotic answer from Jane. Then she moves away from the man and says, 'I've got to go,' and walks off, leaving a confused Alf behind. He's not sure what to do, but eventually he smiles at the old man and then follows her lead.

'Great to see you,' the old man calls after her. 'Don't leave it so long next time.'

Jane quickens her pace; Alf does a slow jog to catch up. Once around the corner, Jane leans back onto the gable end of a building. She is hyperventilating and then starts to cry.

'He seems like a nice old man,' says Alf.

'No, Alf, he isn't nice at all.' Alf looks confused. Then Jane says, 'He's a fucking weirdo. When I was a young girl, he used me.' Alf is even more confused, but then Jane adds something that he understands: 'He used to take me to different houses, Alf, and let other men fuck me.' Alf doesn't know what to say. Then he feels like vomiting when Jane adds, 'And he's my grandad – how messed up is that?' She continues, 'I'm sure he was part of some ring.'

Alf is in shock and says nothing, but he instinctively puts a supportive hand on Jane's shoulder.

29

Mike and Ted decide to try Elton again. They use the bus, train and taxi, except this time they tell the taxi driver to wait, in case they get another short answer from Elton.

Much like before, they get so far with Elton and then he says, 'I don't think so. Fuck off.'

They make their way back the same way they came.

30

For the first time in his life, Jez is starting to feel like he has a place in this world. He has no problem getting into clubs now. In fact, he is well known in six places, where entry with the security teams is a wink and a nod, but with the bar staff it's 'Hey, Jez' and the late-teen and early-twenty-something females call him 'Jezzie baby'. There aren't that many in his new network that are his age; in fact, he hasn't met anyone his age – most are in their late twenties, and there are some really old people in their early forties. Kenny's firm informally calls itself Manhattan for no reason that Jez understands; after all, none of the people he's met are American.

He likes Kenny, who treats him well, and the pocket money is serious. It's pocket money in name only; in reality it's more like a wage. Kenny has advised him that if he ever gets caught by the police with anything on him, he's to say nothing, just phone him on a particular number and then he'll organise legal representation, and because he's sixteen, he'll be fine. Jez queried if it would land him back in Feltham, but Kenny said that getting caught with drugs wouldn't see him sent back, that it would only happen if he got caught for violence, and that that would definitely get him banged up back inside. Jez is taking his word on this.

Jez doesn't mind helping people to party. He sees how ecstasy and cocaine make some people high and happy and he thinks that's a good thing. Kenny has advised him why under no circumstances should he ever use heroin. However what Jez finds most weird is how many people are into a horse anaesthetic called ketamine.

Lots of girls are interested in Jez now, and he's been having a laugh with a few of them, but then he meets Zafia Morgan. Zafia is just there in front of him, dancing in the club, and boom, he has fireworks going off in his head. She's special, there's something about her; it's an *Oh my God* moment like he's never had before.

31

Bel is very confused. Johnson brought her to his flat and when they had finished having sex, he introduced her to someone else at the flat and asked her to have sex with him too. She felt uncomfortable about this, but Johnson said, 'He's my friend. If you love me, you will.' She didn't relinquish her discomfort over the situation, but felt like she should do what Johnson asked, so she had sex with this other guy.

Bel thought it was a one-off, but since then, in the last few weeks, Johnson has asked her to have sex with others too and he's become more distanced from her. She's hardly having any sex with Johnson now. He still refers to her as his woman, which she accepts must mean something, but he doesn't say that he loves her anymore, and she doesn't really like any of the guys she's now having sex with.

Bel is a serious snooper – if any child was ever destined to work for MI5, it's her. The staff have certainly noticed this trait. The staff office generally has an open-door policy to facilitate good communication between the staff and the children, but they have had to make sure that office cabinets containing confidential information are always locked, to stop Bel from having a nosey about. Bel has been told off for being nosey, but words are just words and they don't appear to have any impact on her. Bel has snooped around all the other children's bedrooms at different times. These aren't always locked, apart from Jez's – his is always locked, but he has a temper too, so it might not be the smartest thing for her to snoop there anyway.

Today Bel is having a lazy look around Danni's room. She has a look in the wardrobe – she recognises the clothes; checks the chest of drawers – socks and underwear, nothing out of the ordinary, and she's seen some of these on the clothesline too. There's some cheap jewellery and some old toys, an old doll, and then she finds something that triggers her curiosity: letters. She sits down and goes through these. It's then that Danni arrives in the room and catches Bel red-handed.

She snatches the letters out of Bel's hand. 'What are you doing? These letters are private.'

'So, your mum's in Holloway Prison?'

'You bitch.'

'Chill, sister.'

'I am not your fucking sister. Get out.'

Bel rises up from where she is sitting and gives Danni a wide berth as she goes around her.

'My mum messed up, that's all,' Danni confidently retaliates.

Flatly, Bel responds, 'At least you have a mum.'

32

One of the duties of a project worker is to help the children to tidy their rooms. Not to do it for them – it has to be a joint thing. It's Gary's week for this task and he has helped Jane and Alf. He really wants to just tick the box for this boring task and get it out of the way, and he doesn't take Jez's absence as the obstacle that it is. Rather than wait to do the task with Jez, he decides to do it for him.

He uses the master key to gain access to the locked room. The room isn't untidy and is relatively clean. Gary has a nosey about. He doesn't like Jez; he views him as a nasty asshole. Age doesn't come into it, and there aren't that many years between them. Gary's view is that Jez needs a box in the mouth, but he and the other staff aren't allowed to do it. It's a sackable offence, and a crime.

Stealing money is also a crime, but that doesn't stop Gary when he comes across a pile of money. It's in a shoebox at the bottom and back of the wardrobe. Gary counts it out: four thousand pounds. He takes three thousand out and then puts the box back where he found it. He looks around the room to try to work out if he has moved anything. He hasn't. He quietly opens Jez's bedroom door – the coast is clear. He closes it behind him and heads downstairs.

33

Sarah George is Laura Giggs' community mental health nurse. She has been visiting Laura on a weekly basis since the alert from Dr Irene Nolan. She thinks Laura is a little bit more elated than she has been for some time, but Laura isn't actually elated, the observed behaviours are to do with sleep deprivation. Sarah hasn't had much input with Massie and Donna in the past, but with the regularity of her visits, she's able to compare them to her own children who are of a similar age, and they do come across as less energetic than her pair.

Laura has been to the GP with Massie and Donna twice more recently. On one of these occasions, Dr Nolan reassured her that the children were okay, and on the other occasion, she prescribed some medicines to help them following a bout of diarrhoea. The medical practice receptionist has only seen them in the park once since the last time, and she noted to herself that things seemed to be okay.

34

Melanie is delighted. She has received the financial statement for the home and they are on target for the first time ever. Her bosses are happy. She explains to her team that they're in the black for the first time, that this is good for all of them, that it will help all their futures, that it's good for the security of the home, and that they should use it as a base from which they can work hard for their five children, to help them to make a go of their lives.

This positivity is broken by noise, an argument somewhere else in the house. Jez is angry about his money being stolen. He can't formally do anything about it; it's not like he can tell the police or even go to Melanie – it would require too much explaining. He has noticed that Bel has been getting a lot of new things, though; it must have been her, he thinks. He's got all menacing and aggressive with her and started to make threats.

Danni and Alf are trying to intervene, and the house staff arrive just in time to see Jez push Alf over. That is a serious house rule violation, an act of violence. The staff impose themselves and stop it from escalating any further.

Alf doesn't make a big deal of it, but Bel is frustrated and threatens Jez: 'I know people who'd be very unimpressed by this, Jez. You need to get a grip.'

Jez is still feeling explosive, but he goes to his room as directed by the staff. And as if this isn't enough for Melanie to be dealing with, Mike breaks the news that it looks like Jane is missing again.

The Special Skill

35

Mike had put it off as long as Ted would allow, but things have come to a head: he's going to have to case a bank. Just case it, though, as he still isn't up for robbing one. They agree on the bank. In the event that something goes wrong, and to protect his identity, Ted advises Mike that he should wear a disguise.

Mike gets the bus to Reading, carrying his disguise in a non-identifiable, ordinary white plastic bag. There's a baseball cap, some dark sunglasses and his father's beige raincoat. In a public toilet he changes into this disguise, and then he takes another bus into the town centre.

He steps into the agreed bank. Ted is on his shoulder. He gives a running commentary. He points out that there are five tellers, and that there are also likely to be people in the back office. Mike goes up to one of the tellers and hands over five ten-pound notes and asks in a strange voice if she can give him a fifty. She opens a drawer and as she does, Ted has a good look inside. He does quick arithmetic in his head. Lots of fifty-, twenty- and ten-pound notes. Ted states that there are probably a thousand ten-pound notes, a thousand twenty-pound notes and a hundred fifty-pound notes.

'That's thirty-five grand she has,' he says, 'and there are five tellers, so we're looking at one hundred and seventy-five thousand pounds.'

'What are you on about? We aren't robbing a bank. Look at all the CCTV – it's everywhere.'

'That's why you're disguised, stupid.'

'And do you think they're just going to hand the money over?' says an irritated Mike.

'Of course not,' Ted replies. 'We'll have to use a gun.'

'A gun, have you lost your mind?'

'No, but you said it yourself: they aren't just going to hand the money over.'

'And where will we get a gun?'

'Dad has one. It used to be our great-grandfather's in the war.'

'Why would he have had one?' Mike asks. 'He was an aeroplane mechanic.'

'It probably wasn't his. He probably got it as a keepsake or something.'

'This is crazy. Let's get out of here,' demands Mike.

They head back using the same route, and Mike removes his disguise in the same toilet. By the time they're on the bus back to Bracknell, he's has completely ruled out robbing a bank. Instead, Ted is now trying to manoeuvre him into robbing a bookies, saying that bookies prey on the poor, they target their marketing towards people with gambling problems, and they're rich, undeserving scum, to try to win him over. Mike agrees that bookies are unscrupulous, but his mind is elsewhere.

'What's wrong?' asks Ted.

'It's work. I'm worried about the conflict between Jez and Bel since she stole his money.'

Ted pauses and then seizes his moment. 'If I put your mind at ease about Jez and Bel, will you rob the bookies with me?'

They step off the bus. Ted persists. Mike believes this is just another wild goose chase idea, so he half-heartedly agrees.

Ted gets Mike to sit on a bench. He is in Mike's hand and looks at him eye to eye. 'You can chill with Jez and Bel, because Bel didn't steal the money.'

Mike looks at Ted with distain. *What a tosspot,* he thinks to himself.

Ted reads this and says, 'In fact, it wasn't any of the children.'

'And how do you know that?'

Ted pauses, and then continues, 'Since I returned as this new version of me, I've had a certain skill.' He pauses again. Mike is laughing. Ted talks above the laughter. 'I'm able to kind of read people's minds.' Mike is still laughing. 'I step into their ear, then I can somehow pass through the eardrum and into their middle ear, then, by putting my hand on their stirrup bone, I'm able to access their memory bank.' Mike stops laughing, but he doesn't quite believe what he is hearing. 'I've checked Bel's memory, and the others; they didn't steal his money.'

'I don't believe you.'

'They didn't.'

'That's not the bit I don't believe. What I don't believe is that you have this ability that you say you have.'

'If I prove it to you, will you rob a bookies with me?'

Mike is certain Ted is pranking him, that this is all a hoax, so he says, 'Sure.'

'I expect you'll want me to tell you things that only you and you alone know about you.'

'Of course, exactly.'

Ted then tells him a raft of things. Mike is initially astonished, but he is also an immediate believer; Ted does indeed have the gift he claims to have.

36

Melanie was really worried when Jane and Alf went missing. Initially, there was the concern for their safety, but that abated once they returned and then a different type of worry took over: anxiety about how it looked for the home. It isn't a good look not being able to keep track of the children and not being able to keep them safe. She also felt uncomfortable about doing what she was told to do by her superiors in the company, which was not to notify Ofsted about these events. She didn't sleep for a whole night. Her boss said it could be viewed as doing what was needed for the greater good, as protecting the company's name meant they were able to continue to operate, and in doing so, help more children. Melanie still felt uncomfortable. It felt wrong; it was covering up things, meaning that lessons would never be learnt. But she also needed to be careful of the politics. She had heard stories of other managers who had been pushed out of their roles for not doing what the seniors had wanted. So in the end, and probably for an easy life too, Melanie had decided to comply.

What Melanie doesn't know is that things are even worse than she thought, as Jane has sneaked off to her mother's twice on her own since her adventure with Alf. She's done this on weekends, to avoid being detected as missing from school, and the staff at the home thought she was just out and about in Reading.

Alf noticed she was missing on those days, and he expects that today, another Saturday, Jane will probably head over to her mother's again. He follows her out of the home and asks if he can come. Jane is comfortable with this and agrees.

As before, it's a case of following people through ticket barriers, but it's much more difficult than on a weekday, because without the commuters, it's less crowded. Fewer people go to London on a Saturday.

About a block away from her mother's flat, Jane ducks behind a van that's parked on the side of the street. Alf follows her lead. Jane has spotted some guy in the distance, and even though she isn't sure if it's who she thinks it is, she prefers to play it safe rather than be sorry. She stays out of view and the person passes by on the footpath across the street from them without knowing she and Alf are there. It is who she thought it was, a chap called Ivor. She's pleased that she's avoided meeting him.

Alf asks, 'Is that a person you wanted to avoid?'

'Yes.'

'Who is he?' he asks.

'That's a guy called Ivor. He's one of the paedos that my grandad used to allow to have sex with me.'

Alf nods his head. He doesn't have any words at this moment that he thinks would be useful.

After spending a number of hours with her mum, Jane is quite tired. She doesn't really know why – they didn't do much, they just lay next to each other – but of course at this age, Jane wouldn't really understand the amount of emotional energy she is expending in coming to terms with the situation involving her mum's health. As a result of her tiredness, on the walk back towards Hackney Central her radar is blunted and she encounters Ivor.

'Hello,' he says. 'I heard you'd returned.' Jane is too tired to care but is nervous. Ivor extends his hand towards Alf so they can shake whilst saying, 'Is this your boyfriend?'

Alf initially moves his hand to engage in the act of shaking, but quickly recalls that this man raped Jane when she was a child, so he puts his hand back down by his side. The man looks nonplussed, but Alf is ecstatic when he hears what Jane says to Ivor. 'Yes.'

This is brilliant, thinks Alf, *I have a girlfriend. Jane just said I'm her boyfriend.* It was an emotional high like he had never experienced before, a high of Everest proportions.

37

Jez is seriously on the up. He has become more and more confident in himself week by week. He feels like a somebody now. He has had several dates with Zafia, and one of his new pals in the Manhattan gang loans him a car so he can show off and impress her. Tonight, he's driving her back to near where she lives. She's talking about the future.

'Maybe I'll be a lawyer or maybe a pharmacist like my mum. What about you?'

Jez thinks for a moment, 'Dunno,' he says. Then he smirks and follows up with, 'Maybe I'll do something in sales, pharmaceuticals. I could see me working as a drugs rep.'

He drops her off near her home and then heads out for a spin on his own. On his travels he spies Bel by the side of the road, and he drives up alongside her and encourages her to get in. They drive around.

Jez jests, 'So, I have a car now – are you going to give me what you promised?'

Bel giggles. 'You're too late. I have a boyfriend now.'

Jez chills for a moment and then responds to the smiling Bel, 'What a pity. Are you sure? We don't need to get married, you know, it doesn't need to be serious. I have a girlfriend too.'

Bel says nothing, just keeps smiling. She isn't sure if Jez is being serious or just joking when he says they can be suck buddies.

38

Alf doesn't have a rapport of any kind with Jez. Danni is nice to him, but they never hang out. However, he is pals with Jane, and to a lesser degree Bel. He has never had female friends before. *It's nice,* he thinks.

He and Bel are chilling in the park when a group of six males head in their direction. Bel has been having regular sex with three from this group, set up by Johnson. One of the guys who's been having sex with Bel introduces her to those who haven't met her before. 'This is Johnson's girl.'

'She's sweet,' says one guy and he excitedly clicks his fingers.

A guy who's a stranger to Bel walks up close to her and puts his hand on her bum and says, 'I'm one of Johnson's pals too. I want the same as the others – we can head into the trees.'

The gang laugh. Alf knows something is up, but his radar isn't developed enough for him to understand what's going on.

Bel looks uncomfortable and is worried for Alf's safety. 'Not now. I can meet you at the flat later.'

The guy quickly responds, 'Nah, now, girl,' and catches

her tightly around the upper arm and moves her about half a metre in the direction of the trees.

Alf intervenes firmly, saying, 'Leave her alone.'

The guy turns around and smiles. Then he gives a signal of some kind to the others, who rush Alf and quickly daze him with some punches to the head. He falls to the ground and they kick and stamp on him while the ringleader holds Bel tightly to stop her from intervening. The assault lasts less than a minute and the gang run off when a mother with young kids, Laura Giggs, shouts at them.

Back at the home, Alf is fussed over. He has bruises and cuts and these are treated. The police attend the home, but neither Bel nor Alf volunteers that these males are known to Bel.

Dr Nolan's receptionist saw the event too, but rather than viewing Laura's actions as positive and brave, she frames them as putting the children at risk, and the doctor contacts Laura's community mental health nurse, Sarah George, again.

39

Zafia's parents are keen to meet Jez, but Jez is less than interested. He eventually capitulates, though, as it's important to Zafia because she wants to please and impress her parents.

The dining room is spacious and looks out onto a huge garden. The chairs look expensive and the table is huge and is a shiny wood of some kind. The cloth feels expensive and the cutlery is arty and is referred to as silverware. Jez is on his best behaviour: no swearing, and he makes it look like he is listening. Zafia's mum is chatty, but her dad seems distant; he hardly speaks, he just watches. Zafia is beaming, though.

Jez has lied about the school he goes to. He hasn't even told Zafia he goes to a PRU and instead has talked up the school that Bel and Jane attend, leaving the impression that this is where he goes too.

The mum engages him. 'Zafia said you might be interested in working in the pharma industry. I might be able to put in a good word for you. Are you studying chemistry?'

'No, it's more the sales side than the creation of drugs

that I think I would be good at.'

'Well, when the time is right, I'll help you if I can.'

'Thank you, you're very kind. Zafia already told me so and it's obviously true.'

The mum smiles, Zafia gushes, but the dad just chews away.

After dinner, the dad offers to drive Jez home, but Jez politely declines, saying that he's happy to take the bus. Zafia walks him to a bus stop and waits till he boards, and once he is seated, they exchange waves as the bus pulls away. *Thank fuck that's over,* he thinks to himself. *I wouldn't want to be doing this too often; her dad is a right arse-ache.*

40

Alf's wounds have started to heal. He is in the garden with Gary.

'Why didn't you use what I taught you?' Gary asks.

Alf considers before answering, 'I didn't realise it was going to be a violent situation and I got jumped by about five people too.'

'That's a shit excuse, Alf. You're a monster – look at the size of you, the power you have. You should have anticipated it. Don't wait for them to tell you their intentions, don't waste time waiting for a signal. Control the situation. Strike first, strike hard.'

Alf nods throughout. Then they start on the pads.

Gary continues, 'That's the problem with children's homes: they want you all docile and compliant, that's their ultimate goal, Alf. But fuck that. I'm going to up your training and show you how to do things that I'm not supposed to. I'm going to train you to be the toughest motherfucker ever. No one will mess with you by the time I'm finished with you.'

Alf is delighted. On the inside, he's so pleased. On the outside, he's really going for it; he's putting in one hundred and ten per cent. He believes in Gary.

41

Jez moves his head from side to side as he combs his hair using the mirror in the downstairs hall, to ensure each hair is exactly where it's supposed to be.

Danni, passing by, smiles to herself, and then stops and turns back to him. 'Are you the Jez that Zafia talks about?'

A slightly panicked Jez looks about to see if there is anyone else in the vicinity and if they might have overheard anything. There's no one. He walks towards Danni and, at a low volume, asks, 'What do you mean?'

She explains, 'There's a girl in my class at school and she keeps going on about her dreamboat, Jez. There can't be that many Jezs in this area our age. It's you, isn't it?'

Jez looks around again to make sure they're alone. 'Don't say anything,' he quietly requests.

A slightly confused Danni asks, 'To whom and about what?'

Again, Jez checks no one is around and then turns back to Danni. 'Don't say anything to anyone here about Zafia, and don't pretend to anyone at school, especially Zafia, that you know me.'

Danni can see a vulnerability in Jez she hasn't seen

before. He obviously likes Zafia. She double-checks: 'Zafia doesn't know about you being here?'

Again, Jez looks about. 'No.'

There is a pause and then Danni says, 'I promise she won't hear anything from me.'

Jez is relieved. He gives her a thumbs-up and returns to the mirror and his hair.

42

Third time lucky, think Mike and Ted. *Time to try Elton again.*

Same as before: a bus, a train and a taxi. Again, they ask the taxi driver to wait, but there's no need: they don't go home by taxi this time, as they get arrested by the police for harassing Elton.

They are released without charge on the understanding that they never go near his house again or ever go near him in public. At the police station, Derek speaks up, telling Mike that he needs to take the deal on offer from the police. Ted shrugs his shoulders, then Mike does the same and says, 'Fine.'

43

Jane and Alf are back over in the park. Chilling. Just hanging out. Initially, Alf was on edge, given that he'd been beaten up there a while back, but once he saw that there weren't any gangs about, he was able to relax. He can breathe easy around Jane too. He feels calm in her company. He loves looking at her. He loves her eyes.

They are both lying on the roundabout. Jane is on her back with legs outstretched and bent at the knees, meaning she has both feet on the ground. Alf is lying close by and on his side, looking over at her. Jane is caught by surprise when he asks, 'Do you love me?'

She immediately sits up and looks at him, to try to gauge what he might mean by the question. Is he joking? Does he mean platonically, or love like in boyfriend and girlfriend? She so wasn't expecting this. Alf is her buddy, her pal, someone she can rely on. She tries to quickly work out if she has given him a wrong signal. Her brain quickly tells her she hasn't. She needs to manage this carefully, she thinks.

'How do you mean, Alf?' she asks, trying to gather information.

'Like, am I your boyfriend?'

Shit, she thinks to herself, and then, to try to control the situation, she reaches over and pats him on the shoulder and says warmly, 'No, we're more than that. We're very good friends.'

Alf wasn't expecting this. In his head he had started to imagine they would get married and everything. He feels offended. He stands up and steps off the roundabout. Then, with confusion in his heart, he looks at her and says, 'But you said I was your boyfriend.'

'No, I didn't.'

'Don't lie to me. You did, when we met Ivor.'

Jane hadn't remembered saying this, because at the time she hadn't meant it like that – she'd said it to protect herself, to try to keep Ivor at a distance.

'Yes, I remember now, I did. It was because I was scared.' There is a pause and then she says 'Alf, I'm not into relationships.'

Alf isn't good at processing emotion and it takes an extra moment for him to take on board his interpretation of what Jane said. He points at her and with tears in his eyes shouts, 'You used me.' Then he runs away.

44

Staff at the home have started to escort Jane to and from school to try to control her excursions to wherever it is she goes. This has curbed her gallivanting and as a result she hasn't been to see her mum for four days. *Time is ticking,* she thinks to herself.

Today, after she has entered the school, she walks right through it and out the back gate, and from there she travels to see her mum. She can see a change in her; she's ever so slightly weaker and is beginning to feel pain.

On the way back to the train station she bumps into Ivor. Literally. Her initial reaction is to mutter an 'I'm sorry', but this doesn't fully fall from her lips; she doesn't get past the 's' sound once she realises it's him.

Ivor smiles and reaches out and strokes her cheek whilst saying, 'Look who we have here.' She backs away from him. 'Don't be like that,' he says. 'We're old friends after all.' She feels sick to her stomach. She says nothing, but continues to slowly back away. He takes the rejection badly. 'Fine, be like that, but you aren't really my type anymore. You're a bit too old for me now.' And then he smiles the slimiest of smiles. 'I would love to meet your younger sister, though.'

Jane launches herself at him and he laughs at her onslaught, but the stone of her ring catches him on the cheek and draws blood. This changes his demeanour – he catches hold of her by the jacket using his left hand, and then lines her up for a right-hander to the face, which fully connects and sends her flying.

As she gets her bearings whilst lying on the ground he sneers at her, 'Where is your sister these days?'

Jane doesn't know. *She'll either be in foster care or a children's home,* she thinks.

Ivor reads her well. 'You don't know, do you? Never mind, your grandad will fill me in.'

Jane gets her bearings, and quick as a flash is on her feet and scarpering away. Ivor shouts after her, 'Bye, see you soon.'

45

When Jane arrives back at the house, she manages to sneak in. This is only possible because of the commotion that's currently occurring. Jez and Bel are face to face hurling insult after insult at each other. Four staff members manage to get between the two.

Jez keeps shouting at the staff 'Mind your own business' and 'Don't touch me'.

Mike and Neal remain calm and keep requesting that Jez go to his room. 'No one is touching you,' they repeat.

Gemma gets Bel to her room, and after a few minutes, once she sees that the tearful Bel is safe, she leaves her. She now needs to go and check on Jane, who she saw slink into the house when it was all kicking off.

46

When Gemma reaches Jane's room, the door is closed and Jane doesn't respond to the knocks. Gemma enters and she sees that Alf and Jane are both in Jane's en-suite. Alf is pressing ice he got from the kitchen onto her face to help with the swelling from Ivor's punch.

Gemma says, 'Thanks, Alf, I'll take over,' and she does.

While tending to Jane's face, Gemma asks her, 'So, how is your mum?'

Jane is caught off guard for the second time today. She responds angrily, 'Alf, you dickhead, what have you done?'

Alf has a sincere look of guilt on his face. 'Gemma was worried. You were disrespecting the house. I was angry too, and so I grassed you up.'

Gemma intervenes, 'Actually, it wasn't quite like that, Jane. Alf was worried for your safety and it turns out he was right.'

'You blew your chance, Alf. No way we'll ever be an item now. You can't be trusted. Get out of my room.'

His head drops and he slowly leaves with all the disappointment of a person who's just found their missing multi-million-pound winning lottery ticket all mashed up in the back pocket of their recently washed and dried jeans.

'Don't be like that,' Gemma says warmly to Jane.

'He let me down,' Jane cries out.

'He did good by you. And don't forget, he isn't like the rest of you either – he learns things more slowly. Be kind to him.'

47

Danni hears Bel sobbing in her room. She goes in and comforts her with a hug. Bel says sorry for being distant to her and for the snooping and not being a pal. Tearfully, she tells Danni that she doesn't have any female friends, never has, just doesn't get on with females, and that all her friends are male.

'Men like me,' she says.

'Girls would like you too if you gave them a chance,' is Danni's response.

'Girls are hard work, whereas with boys and men, it's just there between us, we're mates.

'Why is that do you think?' Danni asks.

Bel stops crying. She thinks and then responds with a shrug of the shoulder.

Danni points at Bel's groin. 'It's because of what's between your legs, Bel. You give it out too easily, way too easily. Those blokes aren't your friends. They're using you, Bel. Men will do anything for sex and they've figured out that you deliver.'

Bel is annoyed but keeps it under wraps. Still, she has to defend herself, so she mildly throws a low-level insult at

Danni: 'Sure, Danni, like what do you know?'

In a matter-of-fact way Danni responds, 'A lot actually. My mum used to be a prostitute; she's told me a lot about men.'

48

Mike ends up in Jez's room trying to deescalate him. Ted is bored but in his own way is supportive of Mike, which Mike finds unhelpful. 'Hit him, Mike, don't take shit from this wanker.'

'You aren't helping.'

Ted responds, 'There's no point in me hitting him. I'm a lightweight now.'

'More of a flyweight, if we're being honest.'

Insulted, Ted replies with a snarl, 'You're such a funny man.'

Jez is still wound up tightly. 'I'm so pissed off with Bel. I'm going to cause her harm. She won't get away with this, the bitch.' He keeps saying this over and over.

Eventually, Mike tries a new tactic and says something different to chill Jez, the truth: 'It wasn't Bel.'

This gets Jez's and Ted's attention. Ted says, 'I hope you know what you're doing.'

Jez says, 'It was that dumb fuck Alf, wasn't it?'

'No, it wasn't him either,' says Mike.

'Well, I doubt it was Danni, so what you're saying is that it was Jane. Fair enough, I can see how she would be a fit.'

'No, no, it wasn't her either. It was none of the children here.'

'What? It was someone on the staff?'

'I can neither confirm nor deny. All I will say is that it wasn't one of the other kids.'

'Tell me, Mike, who the fuck was it and how do you know?'

'That's all I'm saying, Jez.'

'I need to know,' he demands.

'Yes, you do, and you're resourceful – I'm sure you can find out who it was if you want. All you need to do is set a trap and catch the culprit in the act.'

49

Gary uses some of the money he stole from Jez to buy some branded trainers. He likes the fact that it's Jez's money that's paid for these given that it was Jez who was belittling him in the first place for wearing non-branded ones. Jez hasn't missed the money per se; he had more than the four grand stashed in his room and has money stashed in other places too and has some in his newly opened first bank account as well. Jez has noticed Gary's footwear, though, and it's got him wondering if it was Gary who nicked his money. He lets it pass, as in truth he suspects everyone, even Melanie, but it reminds him that he needs to set a trap of some kind.

He doesn't give it much thought, as he's busy with his sideline and distracted by Zafia as well, and instead of setting a trap, he buys some spyware instead. He sets up the tiny camera in his room; if you didn't know it was there, there is no way you would see it. It's connected to his mobile. He can see what's going on in his room when he's not in it, and there's a recording facility set up too that kicks in any time a sensor detects certain types of motion in the room.

Gary isn't all bad, though. He's continuing to have a

positive impact on Alf. He has been training him in boxing, and teaching him Israeli special forces martial arts, a thing called Krav Maga. Alf is really psyched about all this. He is half convinced that he could become a world champion in the UFC. This is his new life goal.

50

'I wonder what it's like to be a woman,' says Ted. 'Given that you're able to read people's minds, there's nothing stopping you from going inside a woman's head and understanding it.'

'I've done that already. I understand it a bit, but not enough.' Mike nods. Ted continues, 'I think if I was still alive, I'd dress up as a woman and go out and about and see what it's like.'

'You still could,' says Mike.

'Nah, it wouldn't work. Sure I would get to wear the clothes, but I wouldn't be able to mingle or interact with others; I wouldn't get a real feel for it.'

'I suppose.'

There's a twinkle in Ted's eye. 'I'm putting it on my bucket list.' Mike is nonplussed. Then Ted continues, 'I'm putting it on my list, but with you doing it, so I can see and feel what it's like through you.'

'No fucking way,' is Mike's reaction. 'And it wouldn't work anyway. We're not the same person.'

'We aren't, but you're the closest thing to me that's ever lived. You've got to do it, please. What harm will come from it?'

'No,' is Mike's response.

'Ah, come on, stop being so difficult and negative.'

51

Relations between Jez and Bel haven't thawed. Jez is keeping his powder dry; he won't make peace until he knows for sure, but he holds less animosity towards her. Bel, on the other hand, is really aggrieved with Jez. She has a seething anger.

Bel is walking around town one evening with three members of the gang who have been using her. She sees Jez hanging about. She walks towards him and starts mouthing off at him. Jez doesn't take the bait, as he sees she's in company and he doesn't fancy his chances in a three against one. Despite this, the three blokes, who are around eighteen, lay into Jez. Their reading of the situation is that he's obviously done something to offend Bel, and though they have no respect for Bel, she is their property and Jez is an outsider, so they will fight for her.

Jez is quickly overpowered, but not for long. Quick as a flash, two doormen from a bar-restaurant-nightclub see his predicament and immediately support him. They have telescopic batons, which they flick open, and given that they are fully grown men and trained in the administration of violence, they batter the three guys with Bel – so much so that the four of them quickly run off. Jez is reasonably unhurt and thankful for the backup he received from the doormen. *There are serious perks to being part of Manhattan,* he thinks to himself.

Johnson, who is the leader of the gang that owns Bel, is angry and unimpressed that three of his people were bested by a couple of doormen and a kid from a children's home. He quizzes Bel to understand as much as he can about Jez and she is delighted to fill him in. Johnson doesn't intend to go after the doormen, but he's definitely going to take issue with Jez; it's just a matter of how and when. He thinks to himself, *Zafia might be Jez's Achilles heel, his weak spot. Maybe this is how I'll teach him.*

52

Mike concedes. Ted is delighted. In town, Mike buys a cheap dress, a blonde wig, tights and shoes. He's seen his mother put on lippy lots of time, so he's just going to use some of hers. He shaves his face and his legs too, as Ted said that if he didn't shave his legs, he would just look weird. He applies different types of makeup to his face, but he isn't sure what they are and he thinks he looks a bit strange. He wipes it all off and washes his face. Then he watches a video on YouTube about applying makeup and starts again. This time he looks like most women his age. The lippy was easy to do. The first set of tights ladder. However, Ted had insisted he buy a few pairs as he expected this could happen. The dress is green. The last thing he puts on is the wig.

'You look good,' says Ted. Smiling, he adds, 'I would.'

'Behave,' is Mike's smiley reply.

Ted insists that Mike take some selfies so they can remember this day. Mike refuses initially, but then starts to see the funny side of it all.

Mike needs to sneak out of the house, but despite his best efforts, both parents manage to encounter him at the same time.

His confused father says, 'I didn't realise it was Halloween.'

His mum is drunk and disinhibited so is very honest. 'What the fuck,' are her words.

Mike just keeps moving and gets out of the house as fast as he can without saying anything apart from, 'Laters.'

Then Gertrude cries, and Derek comforts her. 'There, there, it's been a stressful time for him. But in saying that, I don't know what's going on with him. First quitting his job and now this. I'll have a word with him later.'

Mike certainly gets a few strange looks on his street, but once he's on the bus and into Reading, people look at him a bit less. Ted doesn't belittle him; he's enjoying all this too much and the last thing he wants is for the charade to end prematurely. He feigns support and gratitude instead.

'So how do you feel?' he asks.

'Different. A bit uncomfortable to be honest – the low heel is a real balancing act; I don't know how women do it. The dress makes me feel a bit draughty, and all this gunk on my face, it feels, it feels… greasy.'

As they enter a bar Ted reassures him, 'Well, you look great, and thanks for doing this for me, bro. I won't forget it.'

Ted has schooled him: Mike is about to order a pint of Heineken, but then remembers and takes a glass instead. He sits on a high stool at a high table. A bloke approaches and introduces himself as Dave. Mike tells Dave that his name is Mary.

'Nice to meet you, Mary. I hope you don't mind me approaching you and being so forward with what I'm about to say, but here goes. You're a tall lady.'

'I'm six foot one.'

'Cool. I train the women's rugby team here in Reading and we're always looking for new players.'

'I've never played.'

'Well, here's my card. We train twice a week, and beginners are welcome.'

'Okay.'

Once Dave has departed, Ted chips in, 'You would probably be good, but you need to be careful. What if you end up playing for the England women's team and then one day you're running down the wing at Twickenham and your langer falls out.'

'Will you please shut up? I am not going to play rugby for the England women's team. I'm not even going to attend a training session with Dave.'

'Okay, okay, keep your hair on, and what lovely long blonde hair it is too,' says a smiling Ted.

Mike doesn't bite on this. They stay there for about forty minutes and then move on. As Mike leaves he gets a wave from Dave.

The next bar they go into is livelier. The lights are less bright and the music a bit louder. There are lots of groups of people. A couple of guys buy Mike a drink; he requests a G and T. The men stand either side of Mike, and because of the music, they're a little loud. They're a bit tipsy too. One is called Dean and the other Paul.

Ted pipes up, 'I've been inside their heads. Dean is Dean and he's a multi-millionaire software company owner and isn't interested in you. Paul is really called James. He's unhappy in his marriage, lives with her in a three-bedroomed mortgaged house. He sleeps around, likes hookers and wants to ride you.'

'That's gross,' says Mike, and he starts to ignore the

bloke Paul and focuses his attention on Dean only. After a short while Paul moves away and then so does Dean.

Mike is ready to go home, but Ted convinces him to go to a nightclub. Mike finds clubbing boring; he always has as a man and now he does as a woman. He gets a taxi home and receives some weird looks in the rearview mirror from the driver. Mike is unsure whether the chap is concerned for him as a single lady out alone, or whether he likes this single lady. But after stepping inside the driver's head, Ted advises Mike that the driver is actually trying to determine whether Mike is a woman or something else. Mike gets out of the taxi and as he pays the man he says in his normal voice, 'I think I need a shower now; these tights make my balls extra sweaty.'

The man is shocked, but Ted is hysterical with laughter. 'I never thought you had it in you! Brilliant.'

Mike washes the makeup off and takes off all the women's clothes and also the wig. He puts on his boxer shorts and a t-shirt and hits the pillow. It's three a.m. He needs shuteye, as he is working from midday tomorrow.

53

Jane has another dilemma. Her mother has a GP, though she doesn't see him often. He advised Jane's mum that at some stage she would need to go into a hospice, but she isn't inclined to go, and the GP is reluctant to prescribe her heavy analgesics because of the fact she was addicted to heroin in the past. He takes a stand and believes that way Jane's mum will come round to his way of thinking. It's mostly a trust thing with the GP, but he is also convinced that he is totally right. However, it has all, unhelpfully, turned into a stand-off, with neither party being prepared to back down.

Jane's mum ends up asking Jane to help out. Jane approaches Jez and he agrees to sell her some heroin which her mum can use as pain relief. He strongly insists that this deal stays between the two of them, and that she doesn't tell anyone, not even her mum.

In Hackney, though, after a while, Ivor the paedophile becomes aware of Jane supplying her mum. He thinks about how best to use this knowledge. He explores the different kinds of leverage it could bring him, and of course, he wants revenge.

54

Mike wakes later than he expected, and hurriedly does what he needs to do and gets to work bang on time. Everyone is looking at him and smiling. He immediately panics and rushes to a mirror. *Thank God, I wondered for a second if I had the wig or makeup on.* He calms down, but the looks continue and there are giggles.

Danni smiles. 'So, is it Mike or Mylene?'

Bel smiles and asks, 'Are you LGBTQ+?'

Jez smirks. 'I knew you had problems the minute you walked in here.'

Melanie quickly intervenes. 'Leave him alone. Oh, I am sorry, Mike – am I right to call you Mike? Are you a he?'

Mike understands that they somehow know about last night, but he's unsure how to handle it, so he's keeping quiet for now.

Melanie brings him to her office. 'You could have said at the interview, you know. We wouldn't have judged you.'

Mike waits a moment and then asks, 'What is it that you think you know?'

Melanie shows him her phone. The selfie of him as Mary is all over Facebook, LinkedIn and a range of other social media platforms, with the caption, *It's time I told you all?*

'I'm not sure how that happened,' he says to Melanie.

'It's you?'

'Yes.'

'So how do you want us to refer to you? Is it Mike or Mary or she/her?'

'Mike and he/him is fine.'

'You don't need to feel ashamed,' Melanie adds.

Mike is trying to piece everything together in his head. He gets out his own phone. The picture was posted from his phone. Ted must have done it once Mike fell asleep, as part of a prank, he figures out. He thinks about the potential fallout of all of this and the embarrassment. *Fuck,* he thinks. This is actually worse than the parable about spreading rumours, the one where all the pillow feathers are scattered in the breeze. He is furious.

But then he sees all the messages of support across the platforms and just smiles to himself. As he walks back into the house, all the kids are hanging around and staring at him.

'Look,' he says, 'I'm not LGBTQ+, and I've no problem with anyone who is, and I can explain.'

The children start laughing and make a joke about a river in Africa called denial.

55

Gary enjoyed the easy money he nicked from Jez. It slipped through his fingers very quickly, though, like sand. He thought he would keep it as a lump sum that he could dip into every now and again if he was short or just use it as an emergency fund, but he squandered it.

Just like the grizzly bear that knows where the beehive is, he waits for a day when Jez is out, gets the key to his room and returns to the scene of the crime. He laughs to himself when he finds the shoebox is exactly where it was the last time, and with two and a half thousand pounds there in twenty-pound denominations. He thinks to himself, *What a thick fool Jez is.* He counts out the money on the floor and puts two hundred pounds back and the rest into the zipper pocket of his tracksuit top.

Unbeknown to him, Jez is watching it all live. He's fuming. He thinks about enlisting some of his pals from Manhattan to teach Gary a lesson by giving him a serious kicking, but when he calms down, he comes up with a different plan.

He waits two days, until Gary has a day off. Then he meets Melanie and shows her the footage. He also emails it to her and says that he is thinking about putting it on Facebook. That's just an idle threat to force her hand, he won't do that at all, but Melanie doesn't know this.

She engages with her superiors at Better Futures head office. The agreed plan is that Gary needs to be spoken with. He is to be suspended immediately and then sacked, unless of course he resigns, which is the preferred way forward. Better Futures want to keep this out of the public domain; that's what is best for the company's image.

Jez, of course, is asked what he was doing with that amount of money. He knew what he was going to say in advance, and advises Melanie that it wasn't his, that he was merely holding it for a friend. Melanie doesn't believe him, but what can she say? She is also told by Better Futures that Jez's camera needs to be removed. Jez expected this too and says he will agree to this, but only if Gary is sacked. Melanie says that she isn't going to barter with him, to which he replies in that case he will put everything on Facebook. Melanie keeps calm and says that action will be taken and he won't see Gary again, and that this isn't because of anything that Jez has been saying, but that her superiors have made their own decision, and Jez needs to comply.

Gary is phoned and suspended. He then decides to resign. The matter is closed, as Better Futures don't want to involve the police and for obvious reasons neither does Jez.

The following day Melanie tells everyone that Gary has departed. No one really minds apart from Alf; he's gutted, devastated in fact. Jez tells Danni and Jane what really happened. When Bel finds out, she leaks it to Alf, putting her own spin on it, painting Jez as the bad guy. She's hoping that Alf will attack Jez. Alf is angry and confused, but he doesn't strike out.

Jez thanks Mike for giving him the steer which led to his lightbulb moment which led to him catching the fly. Jez is now saying that Mike is an okay guy, even if he is in denial and confused about whether he's a man, a woman or something in between. Mike says nothing at all; he's just expressionless.

Ted, on the other hand, is ecstatic, as he thinks this will give him a way out of Mike's bad books (he's still pissed off with Ted about the whole prank). 'See, it's not so terrible after all. Sure, I pranked you and embarrassed you big style, but it's helped Jez, who used to hate you. He now thinks you aren't so bad after all.'

Mike doesn't agree with that line of argument.

56

It takes a while for Mike to start trusting Ted again. He doesn't fully; it's more a half trust thing now. He's getting there, though; step by step is his approach to building up their relationship again, after being badly let down.

Ted is still going on about doing a robbery. A bookies. Eventually, Mike agrees to case a bookies the same way they did with the bank. It's into Reading again, using the same disguise as before.

Once home, Ted pipes up, 'We have to do it. We can hit that place.'

'I'm not up for it,' says Mike. 'But even if I was, we'd still have problems. I can't drive, and how do we force the teller to hand over the money?'

Ted thinks and calmly points out, 'We have the revolver. Point that at them and they'll comply.'

'But what if they don't respond?'

'Fire a shot into the ceiling, then they will.'

'What? Are you nuts? Now we're firing shots, and where are we getting bullets from?'

'There are bullets with the gun.'

'You're mad. And even so, those bullets are over seventy-five years old; they probably don't work.'

'We can test them in the woods. But let me have a think about the driving bit. I'll figure it out, I promise.'

'Ted, there is something seriously wrong with you. Honestly, there is.'

57

Alf is completely lost now that Gary has left. It has hit his confidence too. Others try to fill the void and take on being the exercise lead for the home, but it isn't the same. Alf had a connection with Gary. Gary believed in him. Gary made him feel like he was a somebody, that he could be strong, feared and admired. That he could be Mr MMA.

Jane is continuing to visit her mother and is supplying her with heroin from Jez. Jane is feeling extra vulnerable on these trips now, which is partly to do with her having got so used to previously having Alf as a big guy beside her. She also has some anxiety about getting caught carrying the heroin. She knows there could be big legal consequences of that. Her mind is racing. *I'd be kicked out of the home. What if I was sent to Feltham or someplace like that? Or to another home up north – that would stop me seeing my mum before she dies.*

Ivor is aware that Jane is around on a regular basis now, and he knows that she's supplying her mother. He wants nothing from Jane, but out of spite he has decided that he's going to cause her problems.

Things move forward between Jez and Bel. They aren't at

war now, but they haven't called a truce either. The guys that use Bel are still keeping tabs on Jez. They're definitely going to strike back at him; they have already decided on that. Without his knowledge, they have been following him, and they now know where Zafia goes to school, and also where she lives. Jez is totally oblivious to all of this.

Danni hasn't betrayed Jez; she is a person who values loyalty. She bumps into Zafia quite a bit at school; they are pals as opposed to friends. Danni thinks it's cute that such different types, Jez and Zafia, are an item. *It's romantic and dramatic.* She is still keeping in touch with her mum by phone and letters. She doesn't visit Holloway Prison, though, as that's how her mum wants it to be.

58

Mike and Ted head to the woods. Ted has learnt that if he pesters and pesters, then eventually Mike will concede. They are there to test the gun. It was loaded at the house. All Mike needs to do is stand about seven metres from a tree and fire.

The gun works, but for one reason or another the bullets don't bang like they do in the movies, it's more of a softer sound, and nothing at all shoots at the tree. The bark remains undamaged.

'The bullets are damaged, or else they're just duds,' says Mike.

'It's good we came out and tested them.'

'That's that then. Thank God – I didn't want to do any of this anyway.'

Ted quickly intervenes: 'Hold your horses. This is all still achievable. Mark Hillier has the right kind of connections; I'm sure he can put out the feelers and get us some bullets. And I've figured out who can be the driver for us too.'

'Who?'

'Your new best friend, Jez.'

'That's taking things too far. He's in my care; I can't be

taking advantage of him like that.'

'Chill, Mike, it's no biggie; he's a criminal already. Christ, you're taking this new job way too seriously. I think I preferred you when you were a geeky IT wannabe.'

59

Laura Giggs is very worried about her children again. She is tearful and feels no one is listening. They are lethargic and have been vomiting. She calls an ambulance and they're taken to A&E. Laura is well known at A&E. She used to be known there years back when she was manic, but in recent times it's due to her being overly worried about the health of her children. On this occasion, Donna and Massie end up being admitted. They are very ill. Laura is both relieved and angry – relieved that they are being cared for, but angry that no one ever listens to her.

The A & E consultant has some suspicions about the children. *Something isn't right here,* he thinks to himself. He contacts Laura's GP and gets some background on Donna and Massie. Dr Nolan's receptionist also gives him her views on Laura and what type of person and mother she is. The A&E consultant makes up his mind and contacts the on-call psychiatrist.

The psychiatrist meets Laura. Afterwards, the psychiatrist and the A&E consultant decide to err on the side of caution. Their view is that Laura is likely to be suffering from something known as Munchausen by proxy, meaning that it's Laura who is somehow harming her children, to get attention for herself. Social services intervene. Laura is prevented from seeing the children and is advised that once they are ready to be discharged from hospital, Donna and Massie will be placed in emergency foster care.

Laura is broken-hearted. She can't believe any of this is happening and denies absolutely every accusation. Her GP, Dr Nolan, can see why the psychiatrist could think this, and her receptionist isn't surprised at all. But one person is convinced that an error of some kind has been made, and that person is Laura's community mental health nurse, Sarah George. Sarah visits Laura at home to assess her mental state, and leaves vowing to help Laura in every way that she can. Sarah knows Laura quite well. She isn't an expert in Munchausen or Munchausen by proxy, and discusses the case with her supervisor.

'Maybe I'm wrong and maybe I was blind or missed something with Laura, but I think she's a good mum.'

The supervisor is sitting on the fence. 'She was always saying things were wrong with the kids, though, and was always pushing them in front of healthcare services. There's no smoke without fire, Sarah.'

'I don't agree,' says Sarah. 'I need to do some digging. I just have to be sure; otherwise I'm failing not only Laura but Donna and Massie too.'

60

Jez gets sent a video on Snapchat. It seriously worries him. It's Zafia. She's tied to a chair and is wearing her school uniform. She's crying. Some people wearing masks and hoodies are also in the video. They're saying things like they're going to teach Jez a lesson and that they're gangbangers.

Jez immediately calls Kenny and explains everything. Kenny says that no one would mess with the Manhattans, that it can't be related to the work Jez does for them, that it must be to do with something else. As a result, he's reluctant to get involved, but he also tells Jez to get back to him.

Jez's head is spinning. He's trying to work out who might be against him. He initially focuses on Gary, but then lets that pass. He and Bel haven't made up, but they're cool. Then he recalls he had a fight with some of her gang – could it be them, he wonders? He gets back to the home and heads straight to Bel's room. She knows nothing about it, but says it's certainly possible that those people she knows might be into him for revenge. She explains they attacked Alf once and that she isn't really in the gang, that she thought she was in a relationship with Johnson, the leader, but now isn't, and that his mates have expectations now that she hangs out with them and has sex with them. Jez isn't shocked. He has heard stories but never encountered those types himself.

He is now extra worried about Zafia. This is way bigger than anything he can deal with. He phones Kenny again. He asks for some backup, as he now knows five addresses at which Zafia might be being held. In the nicest possible way, Kenny says that his outfit can't help – if it isn't related to the drug trade, then it isn't their beef. Jez thinks about going round himself; he could get a loan of a gun from Kenny perhaps. Bel has advised that she has never seen any of the gang with a gun, but that many of them carry a blade. He knows it would be crazy for him to go alone even if he was carrying a gun.

Bel tells him to call the police. For a number of reasons, he can't. Instead, out of desperation and concern he quickly goes to the workplace of Zafia's dad. There are some things that Jez doesn't say to her dad, but he does explain that he has some enemies, that they're bad and that they've kidnapped Zafia. That she is at risk, that they carry blades but not guns. Following Bel's analysis, Jez advises the dad that they are likely to be holding Zafia at one of three addresses.

The dad is calm but quietly furious. He appears to be well connected. He gets on the phone to a senior policeman immediately. Within an hour, the police raid the three addresses. Zafia is found unharmed. At the property where she was being held are four males, aged sixteen to nineteen, who were expecting Jez to turn up, and they have a selection of baseball bats and knifes in situ to teach him a lesson. None of them are shot by the armed police; instead, they are tasered and badly roughed up. Zafia tells the police everything she knows, which doesn't include anything about Jez. Zafia's parents are relieved to have her returned to them safely and are both very clear with her that she is never to have anything to do with Jez again.

'Never ever, Zafia. Jez is dangerous; he's a fake, a liar and is utter scum,' says her dad.

61

Jez apologises to Bel for their falling-out and thanks her for her help in locating Zafia. He tells her that she's better than those people she's hanging out with. The four kidnappers have been held on remand, but Johnson, the leader of this gang, wasn't in on the kidnapping, so Bel is unsure where she stands and whether Johnson and his gang still think that they own her.

Jez is trying to work out for himself if all this means the bad blood between him and those guys is at an end, or if things are just heating up and there's actually more to come.

Zafia's dad said nothing to the police about Jez, and the four kidnappers aren't grassing on anyone and are trying to make out to the police that this is all just a big misunderstanding. Their lawyer has told them to expect a custodial sentence.

62

Mike refuses to be involved in the bookie robbery. 'It's an insane idea. We don't need the money and the risks are way too high.'

They have a very emotional disagreement. Eventually, Ted is very honest with Mike. 'Look, I need the buzz.'

'Buzz? Load up on chocolate, why don't you?'

'Look, you don't understand. I need this kick, I need it to balance out all the horrible shite I see.'

'Like what?'

'Like when I go inside the heads of Alf, Jane, Bel, Jez and Danni for starters. I've seen a lot of the things that they've endured; that kind of stuff gets to a person.'

'No one says you have to go into their heads and be a nosey parker. Just stop going in.'

'Maybe you're right, but I need us to do this robbery, Mike, please.'

Mike is still hesitating, but inside he knows that he will capitulate and end up doing it for his brother.

A few days later, Mike and Ted head back into the woods, and this time they have bullets from Mark Hillier. Everything works. Both get a buzz from the bullets sticking into the wood. They feel powerful. They feel a bit different to how they usually do.

They plan out the raid – well, Ted does; he has it down, he's thought about every detail. Mike totally disagrees with approaching Jez with regards to driving the getaway car. They both agree that it would take too long for Mike to learn how to drive, and taking a taxi would just be asking for trouble – a witness they couldn't trust, someone who could identify them and help the authorities to trace them. Ted suggests shooting the taxi driver afterwards. Mike loses it with him; he doesn't entertain this insane idea at all. Then Mike suggests using their father but without telling him about the robbery, but Ted doesn't believe it's a plausible option.

Then Ted volunteers, 'What about Ellen?'

'Ellen, the hungry one? We aren't going to an eating competition.'

'I know that, but I saw online a while back that she'd been competing as a rally driver.'

'Really?'

'Yes.'

Mike muses on this and says, 'Even so, just because she can drive fast, why would she want to be tied into a robbery?'

'She was a bit of a criminal back in the day, you know. She told me she used to shoplift when she was a teen.'

'Big gap between being a teenage thief and part of an armed robbery gang as an adult.'

'True, but she probably doesn't have much money, so maybe the money will tempt her. I think we should meet her, size her up, and if it feels right, make her an offer.'

63

Sarah George tries to get information on a number of test results for Donna and Massie from the general hospital, but because she isn't next of kin or the kids' social worker, they decline. Laura gives permission and signs a letter agreeing to allow Sarah access to the results, but due to a court injunction, Laura has been stripped of all her rights in relation to making decisions for her children. Dr Nolan, Laura's GP, is more sympathetic towards Sarah, and even though she isn't supposed to share this info, she has it passed to Sarah.

Sarah is academically bright, but her training is in mental health and the biochemistry results mean nothing to her. Her husband, on the other hand, did a biochemistry degree at university, so he is able to interpret them for her and patiently explain every nuance of these results to her. It's still possible that Laura does indeed have something like Munchausen by proxy and is guilty as suspected, but Sarah thinks very differently now, and what her husband has said to her opens up a new line of enquiry for her to pursue.

64

Jez is still working for Kenny but less so; he feels a bit let down by him, and is also starting to question if life as a dealer is the right life for him. He is missing Zafia and one day he's excited to bump into her at one of the clubs he oversees. She doesn't blank him, but is cold towards him and makes it clear that she was unimpressed by all the lies he told her, as well as the danger he put her in. Jez apologises, saying that he didn't know that she would be targeted, and that it was due to a dispute between him and a gang that Bel is tied into and had nothing to do with his dealing at all. She is unimpressed by the dealing too. Her view is that him being a dealer is his choice, and her choice is not having anything to do with someone who deals drugs. She has warmth for him, but is very clear: 'Life is all about choices, Jez.'

Things thaw between Alf and Jane; he couldn't keep up the anger. He has been supporting her again by travelling with her to her mum's. He doesn't know about the heroin, though, as Jane believes it's best not to tell him. Ivor is still on the scene, monitoring and biding his time.

65

Mike asks Ellen out for a meal. He chooses Pizza Hut because there are great 'eat as much as you like' deals. They get on very well. However, she doesn't eat that much.

'Are you not hungry?'

'I've had enough.'

'I thought you would eat more. Ted said you used to eat loads.'

'Did he?'

'Yes, so much so that he thought you had worms.'

She laughs. 'What a dickhead.'

Mike laughs and turns to Ted. 'She has the measure of you.'

Then Ellen continues, 'My parents didn't have much money when I was growing up and there was never enough food. We used to go to food banks and the like. When I was going out with Ted, I was actually really hungry, practically starving. You know, in the past there were times when I was so hungry that I would steal food from supermarkets.'

'There is so much about the country these days that disgusts me,' Mike says.

She drives him home, and then she leans in and kisses

him. 'Thanks for asking me out,' she says.

Mike wasn't expecting any of this, but he realises that he does like her. She opens the door of the car and it's then that Ted shouts out, 'You need to ask her if she'll be the getaway driver for us.'

Mike is unsure now; he's thinking that he wouldn't want to get his probable new girlfriend into trouble.

Ted quickly responds, 'She's a rebel, Mike – goes on marches, has Robin Hood as a hero.'

'Okay, I'll say something to her.' Mike turns to Ellen. 'Are we a couple now?'

'Yes.'

'Cool. In that case, how would you like to rob a bookies with me?'

66

Sarah George meets her patient Laura Giggs at Laura's flat. Laura isn't depressed but is sad and tearful due to not having access to her children.

Sarah asks her, 'Do you ever get bouts of vomiting and diarrhoea?'

'Not often, but yes, every now and again.'

'But with Massie and Donna it was a lot?'

'Yes, I've been very worried about them.'

'The social workers think you've been interfering with them.'

'In what way?'

'They think the diarrhoea and vomiting is because you've been deliberately making them sick; feeding them water from the toilet has been one suggestion.'

'That's crazy! Why would I do that?'

'To get attention and sympathy is their view. I've seen the results of a number of tests done on the girls, and they have high levels of bacteria in their system that correspond with ingesting faecal matter.'

'I don't feed them poo. For fuck's sake, Sarah, what kind of a mother do you think I am?'

'I'm only trying to help.'

'I know. I'm sorry.'

'Is the water plumbed in here correctly?'

'I don't know,' says Laura.

Sarah walks to the sink and turns on the tap. 'It looks okay.' She puts some in a glass. 'It looks clear, it smells okay and it tastes fine.' Sarah just can't work it out. Then she sees some swimming costumes. 'Do you swim as a family?'

'We do.'

'What pool?'

'We don't use the pool; it's too expensive. We go wild swimming; it costs nothing. Yes, the water's cold, but you get used to it.'

'Where do you do this?'

'You go a little past the park and use the river there, and the creek that's just off that.'

Sarah recalls different stories online about the local water company being criticised for the amount of raw sewage they have been releasing into the rivers and waterways. She googles a story and then gets up Google Maps, finds the park and traces the river and creek as described by Laura. *Bingo,* she thinks to herself, as she can see the piping and storm drains that connect the water company's sewerage works with the local river and creek.

'Laura, I think I know what's happened. It's those scumbags at the water company, they're the ones to blame for all of this.'

Austerity Victims

67

Melanie is happy with how things are running at the home. Everything is on an even keel. The children seem to be getting on with each other again. Well, Alf and Jane are tight and Alf isn't in conflict with anyone else. Jez is calmer and seems to be getting on well with Danni, and his relationship with Bel seems more appropriate. Sure, the children still have their problems: Jez is still doing his own thing and is still sneaking out at night, and Alf and Jane are still sneaking off to Hackney on their day trips. But things are good enough.

A few days later, all that completely changes. Jane and Alf are at her mother's. Her mum doesn't have much time left to live, a week to ten days, and she's very grateful for the heroin; it's making a real difference. As Alf and Jane are heading away from the flats, both are on their guard, keen to avoid Ivor. What they don't know is that Ivor has tipped off a local drug gang that Jane and Alf have been bringing heroin onto their patch. Five members of the gang make to attack the pair. There are two baseball bats visible.

Alf isn't scared; he's up for it. He has Gary in his mind, bigging him up, and he puts the moves he's practised to good use. He really does have the makings of an MMA champ after all. He bashes the five of them. They are totally unprepared for this; psychologically, they were prepared for an easy domination of Alf and Jane.

Then one of the gang pulls out a knife. He runs at Alf, but Alf quickly moves to the side and catches hold of the guy's arm, twisting it until it snaps. The blade falls to the ground. Alf picks up the blade.

Another one of the guys swings a baseball bat at Alf, but Alf is able to move out of the way, and he swiftly retaliates with a punch to the guy's chest – except it isn't an ordinary punch, as Alf is holding the blade in that hand. The guy immediately slumps to the ground and there is blood gushing everywhere. The others flee.

Then there are sirens in the distance. Jane is frozen still. Alf looks at the guy on the ground. He is unconscious now.

Alf drops the blade and turns to Jane and cries, 'I think I've killed him! I was only trying to look out for you. I hope Melanie won't kick me out of the house.' To himself, he admits, *Gary was right. I am good at MMA.*

The ambulance crew aren't able to save the guy who was stabbed. He dies at the scene. The paramedics speak to each other. They agree that there are far too many stabbings and killings these days. They strongly believe that closing down community centres and libraries has had an impact. One of them advises the other that six hundred youth centres were closed between 2012 and 2016. 'That's austerity for you,' he says.

The other adds , 'David Cameron and George Osborne

are the architects of so much violence and death.'

His colleague nods. 'Yes, their hands are covered in blood.'

The police arrest Alf and take him into custody. He will never return to the children's home. Jane is held for a short while as a witness, and once the police have a statement from her, they transport her back to the home.

Melanie is in tears. She's tough, but being tough doesn't mean you don't feel sadness. *Poor Alf, and that poor guy who died. Poor Jane.* Then she starts to think about the home. What will Better Futures think? and what about Ofsted?

68

There is a lot of disappointment at the home. The staff are devastated about what has happened to Alf. Melanie is gutted for Alf, but is also very worried about what will happen to the home. However, it seems that the police aren't interested in the home, because they have the perpetrator, and Better Futures are reasonably chilled and supportive of Melanie. What she doesn't know, though, is that Better Futures have decided that if there is too much attention, they will just sack Melanie and release a public relations statement blaming her, saying that it was a local leadership issue. They believe that removing her will lead to immediate improvements.

Jez is cool about the Alf thing, as he knows he'll be fine at Feltham. He's just hung up on not having Zafia in his life. Bel is worrying about Johnson. She hasn't seen or heard from him and is hoping he's forgotten about her. Danni is taking all the chaos in. She feels for Alf, she feels for Jez, but mostly she feels for Jane, poor Jane, whose mother has died. Jane is devastated. She isn't thinking about the whole Alf thing right now, she's just gutted about losing her mum. 'Life is so unfair,' she cries.

69

Ellen and Mike go through the plan hatched by Mike and Ted. She likes it. They walk and drive through it too, using her car. She agrees that everything should work out fine. She's a bit unsure about having bullets in the gun, but Mike persuades her with a passionate kiss and she concedes, but only as long as he agrees not to shoot anyone. The robbery is planned for the following evening. All they need now is a getaway car. Mike, with his inappropriately placed newfound machismo, says he will sort it out.

He goes to a local Tesco car park with a long tool he got from Mark Hillier, the kind that can be used to open cars without a key. He's very nervous but manages to break into a car and sits in the front seat. He's about to close the door when he's prevented from doing so by a man in a suit who flashes a badge. It's a police detective. He was in the car behind Mike and couldn't believe what he was seeing.

Mike is arrested, but Derek is able to pull some strings with his contacts at the local Chamber of Commerce. Citing the pressure on Mike since the death of his brother, which can also be evidenced by the identity confusion stuff on Facebook, he is able to persuade the police not to press charges. The owner of the car is fine with this, as the car is undamaged.

Once home, an exasperated Derek asks, 'What's going on, Mike?'

Mike says nothing, just shrugs his shoulders. Gertrude takes no notice, as she's a bit comatose.

If this was a warning from the gods of some sort, Mike doesn't heed it. Ted thinks he was a complete numpty for getting caught, but Mike isn't taking the blame, saying that Ted was to blame too as he was a shite lookout.

Ellen thinks it's hilarious. 'Don't worry,' she says, 'I'll steal us a car,' and she does.

Two evenings later, she picks Mike up in a blue Golf GTI, with fake plates. They are ready to rumble.

70

Ellen parks a little down from the bookies. Mike is wearing a disguise. He's sweating.

Ted is ecstatic. 'This is great. I'm buzzing.'

Mike is dressed as an Arab. It's a costume his dad used at a Halloween party twenty years earlier. His face is covered with the headdress and he's wearing sunglasses. He stares into the bookies through the glass in the door. There's one punter in there and another guy in his fifties is behind the counter. Mike calmly walks in, throws the bag on the counter, points the gun at the man and tells him, 'Fill it.'

'You're so cool,' squeals Ted.

The man complies. He then hands over the bag. The punter sees what's going on but looks the other way. Mike walks back to the door and opens it with his gloved hand. He jogs to the car and jumps in. Ted is screaming, 'Drive, drive, drive,' which Ellen can't hear, but she doesn't need any direction. She slowly pulls out and carefully drives off. She uses the indicators properly and three miles later, without attracting any attention, she pulls into a disused industrial estate.

They both get out of the Golf. Ellen opens the boot. She

takes out a petrol canister. She douses the car in petrol and then throws the empty can, the gloves and the hat she was wearing onto the driver's seat. Mike chucks in the Arab costume, the glasses and his gloves. Ellen then sets the car alight and they walk away.

After three hundred metres, they go through a gap in a fence, then they walk through some side streets and stop when they come to a housing estate. Ellen's car is there. They get into it and drive back to her flat. Once inside, they count the money: forty thousand pounds. They split it fifty/fifty as agreed. Then they have sex.

Afterwards, Ellen asks, 'If we end up with a child, what will we call it?'

Mike says nothing; he is dumbstruck at the fact he just had sex. Ted, laughing, chips in, 'Tell her Clyde if it's a boy and Bonnie if it's a girl,' and then Mike laughs too, which Ellen doesn't understand.

71

A couple of days later, Mike is a bit sheepish when the robbery comes on the news at the children's home. The kids and Melanie are glued to it. No one says anything much, as they're all a bit distracted by the other recent events, especially Alf getting arrested.

Jez takes Danni to one side and shows her an article in a local newspaper. Then they google the story and watch some videos. It's a story about a local woman, Laura Giggs, who had her children taken away from her, but they've now been returned. She was accused of harming them because they'd become really ill, but actually they were ill because they'd contracted E. coli from the local river, as the water company had been constantly discharging untreated sewage into the waterways.

'That's terrible. These companies are disgusting,' says Danni.

'They sure are,' says Jez. 'But look at the picture of the CEO of the water company.'

'And?'

Jez explains, 'That's Zafia's father. The cheek of the guy, accusing me of being a criminal and what he's doing is far worse. That's the problem with this country: the real criminals get protected because they wear suits.'

'Poor Zafia,' says Danni.

'I miss her. I love her,' says Jez.

Danni smiles.

72

Some time passes. Ted is bored again. He's thinking about what he wants to do next on his bucket list. Mike and Ellen have cooled things a little and neither has spent any of their stolen money.

Johnson has introduced more new guys to Bel and this has dented her already non-existent self-esteem. She was hoping this was all behind her.

Danni decides to take a trip to London. She visits her mum in Holloway Prison, even though her mum was really unhappy about the proposed visit.

Jane is feeling depressed and is consumed with worry about her younger sister, who is in care somewhere else.

Jez has stopped dealing, but Zafia is forbidden from seeing him, and even though it tugs on her heartstrings, she won't go against her father.

Mike's mother is hard at it, hitting the Bacardi bottle as much as a person can, and his dad just comes across as a lost soul. On the surface everything looks just as it's always been with Derek, but underneath that, things are really wrong. Life hasn't panned out like he thought it would; in fact, nothing has panned out how he had hoped, nothing, absolutely nothing.

Melanie is relieved, meanwhile, as she thinks she has ridden the storm that never came, but there haven't been any referrals for the empty room that was once occupied by Alf. Better Futures have noted this, and are still thinking about whether or not to terminate Melanie's contract.

Then it arrives, a letter for Danni. She shows it to Jez. 'Look where I'll be going .'

Jez asks in astonishment, 'What are you up to?'

'Let's see if I can help you.'

73

A week later, in her school uniform, Danni enters the offices of the water company.

'Hello, I have an appointment to see the CEO, Sebastian Morgan, please.'

She waits in the reception area and then five minutes later is taken to the CEO's office. He steps out from behind his desk and shakes her hand, and then they both sit, just as his personal assistant closes the door behind her as she exits.

'Very nice to meet you, Danni. You go to the same school as my daughter Zafia. Do you know her?'

'I know her a little.'

'And you're doing a project that you think I can help with?'

'That's correct.'

'Well, we run a very successful company here. We make a lot of profit, which keeps the shareholders happy and –'

Danni interrupts him: 'I'm not impressed by your company, Mr Morgan. In fact, I think it's a disgrace, what with it polluting our waterways with human excrement.'

Sebastian is caught off guard. Danni continues, 'And yes,

I am here for your assistance with a project, but the project isn't anything to do with your company, it's to do with your daughter and her ex-boyfriend.'

Sebastian hardens his exterior, becoming more officious and colder. Looking at his watch, he says, 'Is that the time already? Do run along – you'll be late for class.'

'I don't think so,' says a steely Danni.

'Look,' he says, 'it's great that Zafia has a friend who wants to help her in this way, but sorry, no, mind your own business.'

'It's my business not because of Zafia, but because I'm a friend of Jez's.'

This antagonises Sebastian. 'Jez is scum. It's up to your parents to decide who you hang out with, but my daughter won't be having anything to do with him.' He stands up, arrows one of his arms towards the door and says, 'Thank you and good day.'

Danni doesn't budge. 'Mr Morgan, will you kindly sit.'

'I will not.'

'Fine,' she says. 'Maybe I can convince you to soften your stance on Zafia and Jez.'

'I think not. Leave now, or I'll call security.'

'Call them if you like, but it might be better if you listen to what I have to say first, because I'm giving you an opportunity to influence how the shit will hit the fan in your home life. But of course, it's entirely up to you, Sebastian.'

Annoyed but also impressed with Danni's nerve, he folds his arms and sits back down. 'You have two minutes,' he says.

She continues, 'You used to work for a PR company in the Mayfair area of London?'

'Yes, but I've worked for the water company for several years now.'

'I can see how a company that flushes shit into waterways would benefit from having a PR expert.' Before he interjects, she asks another question: 'Have you ever heard of a woman called Nelly Nickers?'

He's ever so slightly flustered, and to buy himself some time, he starts to play with his cufflinks. Then, without much confidence, he denies knowing anyone with that name.

'She says she knows you.'

'I have nothing more to say on this,' he says.

'Nelly – not her real name, by the way – says she knew you very well, that she used to meet you for sex on a weekly basis for about a year.'

'I have never had a girlfriend called Nelly.'

'Nelly never said she was your girlfriend. You used to pay her.'

'I have never paid for sex.'

'She says you did.'

'You think you can come in here and blackmail me about some made-up dalliance I had with a prostitute called Nelly, in the hope that I'll allow my daughter to couple up with some drug dealer you're friends with? You're off your tiny little head, girl.'

Danni remains composed. 'He isn't a drug dealer anymore. And I bet your wife won't be impressed that while she was pregnant with Zafia, you were paying Nelly for sex.'

'You think my wife would believe some hooker called Nelly over me?'

'There's proof.'

'Your time is up,' he says. Then he scoffs, 'Proof, like her word against mine? I think not.'

'DNA proof.'

He laughs. 'Like on a dress? This is so Bill Clinton.'

There's a moment of silence. Then Danni calmly says, 'The DNA is sitting right here before you. I am the proof. My mother only ever told me that my father was a guy called Sebastian who worked in PR. Years later when I understood she was a sex worker, I thought she was probably lying to me about you, that it was all some sort of glamorous but feasible cover story. But then one day Jez said that I reminded him of Zafia, and then I saw you in the papers. Sebastian, the water company CEO who used to work in PR. So I went to see my mum, Mary Chapman. You know that was her real name, she told me you would. Anyway, Mum confirmed it all.'

Sebastian is quiet. Then he says, 'This is all a lie. You're wasting your time. I'm sorry that someone's misinformed you.'

'My mother isn't looking for money from you, Sebastian. If she wanted that, I think she would have been in touch by now, don't you? And I want absolutely nothing from you either. I bet I could sell my story, though, or at the very least put it online. Your wife would leave you eventually, wouldn't she? And the shareholders would release you at some stage too. You know all this. But it doesn't have to be that way, Sebastian. It can all remain a secret, between me, you and Nelly Nickers.' Then she smiles, but her internal smile, which no one can see, is so much bigger.

74

The navy-suited man with the black shoes, white shirt and blue Windsor knotted tie, stands at one end of a large function room, in a not-to-be-disclosed well-known London hotel. He's wearing a microphone to ensure that the ninety people in attendance will hear him when it matters. He has the ability to be heard in such a space without a microphone, but he's known for his emotional intelligence and ability to engage, connect, manoeuvre and manipulate a crowd, and to do so properly requires him to talk quietly and even whisper at times for effect, and without the microphone such aspects of his rhetoric would be lost. He's tall, about six foot two, and strong and fit looking, but doesn't come across as a gym junkie. He has a tight haircut and a scar on the left side of his head that reaches from his temple down to his jaw. With charisma, he addresses the crowd.

'Welcome, welcome, welcome. I'm John Richards and you, my friends, have come to the right place. We'll spend the next four weekends together. We will analyse, practise, explore purpose, appropriately apportion blame and find solutions, and I promise you that by the time you walk out the door there, you'll be the biggest, baddest, most toxic bastards alive.'

The crowd cheer. Then John eggs them on: 'What do you want to be?'

'Bastards,' they shout.

He responds, 'I can't hear you. What is it you want to be?'

They shout it even louder: 'Bastards.'

He acts impressed. 'And what kind?' he asks.

There are different responses, with almost half saying '*the worst*' and the other half saying '*the best*'.

'Okay,' he says, 'I'm going to divide you up into little working groups, fifteen groups of six. Serious consideration has gone into deciding who is in each group, so we can test you and help you to get the best out of yourselves and each other. Now please look at the lists on the walls, join your group and do some introductions.'

The room becomes a hive of activity as everyone starts talking in their respective groups. After about ten minutes, John calls out for silence. He waits and allows the silence to hold, and then he calmly speaks.

'So, the first task of the day is this. In your groups, I want you to discuss what the main problems are in society these days and how we should fix them. Take notes, and then I'll need one person from each group to feed back to the wider group. Have you got that?'

There are lots of heads nodding; a few say '*yes*', a few make an affirmative noise and others say, '*Yes, John.*'

For the best part of twenty minutes, John just sits back and observes. Then he tells everyone they have one minute to get ready to give feedback.

'So group one, what is it you have to feed back? What

are the current problems in society?'

An ordinary-looking man in his early thirties steps forward. 'Hello, everyone. Our group, we think that the main problem is that there are too many people in this country who are just looking for handouts and benefits. They're lazy and stupid. They argue that they have kids to feed, but they made those kids without ever planning how to pay for them, and now they expect everyone else, us hard-working folk, to pick up the bill on their behalf. Well, we say, no more.'

There are cheers and claps from elsewhere.

'Thank you,' says John. Then he scans the room and points at a group of people. 'Group eight, what say you?'

A white woman in her forties steps forward and in a mousey voice says, 'The problem is illegal immigration. We have criminals who turn up on our shores in dinghies. We should blow them out of the water.'

There is a huge cheer, with some shouting supportively, 'Right on.'

John says, 'Group fourteen, please.'

A black man with a British accent speaks: 'We agree with what the other groups have said, but in addition, we think the problems are to do with those people who keep saying that climate change is an issue and that fossil fuels are to blame. What nonsense. There's been climate change since the beginning of time; it's a cycle. We must not give in to these liars who spread fake news.'

There are cheers, but not as many as for the dinghy woman.

At the end of the weekend, John sets them some homework tasks that they must deliver on before they meet again next Saturday. 'In your teams, what I want you to do is go out there and cause problems and chaos, and then when you're back here next Saturday, you'll feed back on what exactly you did. Previous groups have done things to foreigners, targeted the NHS, targeted abortion clinics. Be creative, think out of the box.'

Then he stands still. 'It has been my pleasure to host you this weekend. You've been brilliant; you're exactly what this country needs. Well done for being you.' He gets a loud round of applause.

75

It's Mike's cooking day at the home; it's his signature dish again, spaghetti bolognese. The kids and other staff members are taking the mickey out of him. They know he has a good sense of humour, and given that this is his best dish and really good, they enjoy saying things like:

'Bolognese again, God help us.'

'Whose night, is it? Mike's. Well, it's going to be bolognese, I suppose.'

'Oh no, not spaghetti again.'

Then they all tuck in and it's so yummy that there's zero talking taking place. Mike's mobile vibrates in his pocket. He takes it out; it's a call from his father. He gets up from the table and goes to stand in the corner next to the window. He's only taking the call because it's very unusual for his dad to phone him.

'Hi, Dad,' he says.

'Mike, I'm at the hospital. It's your mother. She's taken an overdose.'

Mike immediately tells everyone he's got to go. He rushes to get his coat.

'Ted, did you hear that?' A concerned and nervous Ted

nods. They stand outside the house while Mike waits for the Uber he has ordered to turn up.

Mike turns up at the A&E department that he previously attended, hoping then that his brother would survive, and given that he didn't, he's filled with dread regarding his mum. His mother is alive. She took a load of pills, paracetamol and ibuprofen. She's been treated and has had her stomach pumped and has been moved to a ward. She will need some liver tests, but the view is that the pills won't have had enough time to damage her liver – a liver that her family expect isn't in good nick anyway, given how much she drinks.

Mike asks his dad, 'What happened?'

'I found her in her room. I wouldn't have checked on her; it was only that I was angry about something and wanted to speak with her about it. It looks like the thing I wanted to talk with her about tipped her over the edge.'

'What's that, Dad?'

'The man who killed your brother... well, there's no case to answer.'

Ted is outraged. 'What the fuck? Some guy runs me over and gets off?'

Mike ignores Ted. 'I'm confused, Dad.'

'So am I, son, so am I. I can't believe it.'

Ted kicks out at Mike, but obviously Mike can't feel anything much given that Ted is so tiny. 'This is so unfair,' Ted says.

Derek continues, 'I heard from the police today. They said the CPS have dropped the case – no evidence.'

'No evidence? This was a slam dunk, that's what we were told,' says Mike.

Derek nods.

Gertrude has woken up and she reaches out. Mike responds and clasps her hand in his.

Ted pipes up, 'Mike, we need answers. Let's get ourselves over to the police station now and catch up with the detective we met there before.'

'Okay.' Mike turns to his parents. 'Look, I need to head off for a short while. I'll see you later.'

76

Down at the station, after about thirty minutes, the junior detective who has been dealing with Ted's case returns to base, out of courtesy, to meet Mike. He was doing something at the courthouse, but didn't really need to be there; one of his seniors there can deliver the necessary on his behalf. He's a young detective, in his early thirties, Detective Constable Sullivan. He shakes Mike's hand and leads him to an empty interrogation room and they sit down opposite each other.

'What happened?' asks Mike.

'I'm really sorry, Mike.'

'What happened?' Mike asks again.

'The CPS and others decided to drop the case.'

'But why? It was a slam dunk, you said so yourself.'

'I don't know the ins and outs of it, just that the decision was taken. It happens like this every now and again unfortunately.'

'But you visited us, told me and my parents that it was an easy case to win and that the guy who did this would pay.'

'I'm sorry, Mike, I really am.'

'But the evidence?'

'That would have been reviewed as part of the process.'

'I'm shocked.'

'This is a fucking scandal,' shouts Ted, 'a fucking scandal.'

'How did this guy get off?' Mike asks. 'A good lawyer?'

The uncomfortable detective responds, 'A good lawyer is always a help.'

'Someone has been paid off. Tell him, Mike – it's corruption,' roars Ted.

Mike says, 'If Ted was here, he'd be shouting about payoffs and corruption.'

'I'm not aware of anything like that,' the detective says.

After a few minutes, the meeting is pretty much at an end and DC Sullivan walks Mike out of the building.

'This is it then?' asks Mike.

The detective nods.

Ted pipes up, 'Inside, he said something about this type of thing happening every now and then and that it's unfortunate. Ask him what he meant.'

Mike does.

The detective is a bit uncomfortable and has to look over his shoulder before quietly replying, 'When you're dealing with someone like the alleged suspect is, there's always a chance that it isn't going to go anywhere.' Mike looks confused and asks, ' sorry detective, you will have to spell it out for me, what is so special about the person that killed my brother?' The detective looks over his shoulder again and follows up with, ' he is a Tory.'

'What does he mean by that?' screeches Ted. 'Tell him, Mike, tell him we're Tories too.'

Mike waits a beat and then responds to the detective: 'What do you mean? Because we're Tories too.'

'Look, Mike, you're a nice guy, but there are Tories and

then there are Tories. There isn't much else I can say.'

Then he departs, and so do the brothers, with Ted saying, 'Fuck this, Mike, fuck this.'

Once home, they find their dad in the lounge sitting quietly on his own in what looks like deep thought. 'Your mother will be discharged tomorrow. They'll keep her in tonight.'

'Okay,' is Mike's response.

'Are you okay?' asks Derek.

'No, not really.'

'Same.'

Then Mikes recounts the encounter he had with the detective and asks his dad, 'What did he mean by that, Dad? We are Tories, aren't we? We always vote Tory.'

'Yes,' says Derek. There's a pause before he adds, 'Maybe what he was referring to is that the Tory who hit your brother was a Tory grandee.'

'What? And because of that, the rules are different or don't apply to him?'

'Yes, I think that's what he might have been suggesting to you.'

A confused Mike asks another question: 'And is that the case, Dad?'

Derek pauses again before calmly saying, 'I don't know, son. Maybe it is, maybe it is.'

An apoplectic Ted says, 'Fuck this.'

77

Mike returns to work and explains everything that's happened to his colleagues. Many have sympathy for him.

Two weeks later, Mike receives a typed letter in the post. It's anonymous and unsigned. The writer says that they were sorry to hear about Ted's case being dropped, and that in their view it was because the killer is a Tory grandee, a person of significant privilege. The writer also says that it came as no surprise to them and that things are far, far worse than anyone understands. They say that if Mike wants to know how it really is, and what being a Tory really means, then he should phone the attached number and talk with an anonymous insider.

Mike isn't sure what the next steps should be, but Ted is crystal in his clarity. 'It's time to put an end to our bucket lists and do something really important. We need to figure out how things really work in this country, and how the person who killed me can so easily evade justice.'

Mike is quietly supportive, but is already half beaten and doesn't have the same energy as Ted for the task. But Ted pushes it: 'I was your only brother, we were a duo. Someone did this to us, Mike – let's fuck 'em.'

After a week, Mike is starting to be ground down by Ted, but he's reluctant to resign from the children's home just to go on this quest, a quest that will probably lead nowhere. He also has a sense of duty to the children now. But then Ted makes him a super offer.

'Look, Mike, Danni is fine. I've been inside her head and she's a great kid, and now that she knows who her dad is, she's turned another corner in her life. Jez, yes, he has his issues, but he isn't a lost cause. However, Jane and Bel are a mess, a total mess to be honest. It saddens me. You know I can go into people's heads and see their memories and understand them, but I think I also have the ability to fix people, to help them to deal with their past and to put the problems it has caused, to bed. If I do this for these kids, will you resign from here and help me catch my killer?'

Mike is gobsmacked. He knows Ted has amazing talents, but surely not this ability. *If Ted is telling me the truth, then he really is exceptionally extraordinary,* he thinks to himself. 'You can heal the mind?'

'I think so.'

'That's amazing – you're amazing. I'm so proud of you. If you can do that for them, wow, that would be something special.'

'If I do it, will you join me?'

Mike thinks for a few further moments. 'If you do it and it works, then yes, but only if it works.'

Ted agrees to this. They head closer to Jez. Mike helps Ted to get really near to Jez, and then Ted calmly heads into his middle ear. Once there he places his hand on the stirrup bone, closes his eyes and concentrates hard. After twenty minutes, he comes back out.

'One down, two to go,' he advises.

Mike takes Ted to Jane, and again Ted places his hand on the stirrup bone, staying in her ear for forty minutes. Once out, he says, 'Two down, one to go.'

Then it's the same again with Bel, but with her, it takes an hour. When he comes out of Bel's ear, Ted is very upset; he is bawling, crying.

Mike consoles him. 'What's wrong, Ted, what's wrong?'

In between the tears Ted says, 'Man, if you could get inside their heads like I did and see what I saw, you'd cry too. I'm just overcome by it all. Life is so cruel sometimes.'

'Do you think it worked?'

'I think so,' Ted replies. 'I suppose we'll see soon enough.'

They wait, and after a few days it becomes clear that Ted's interventions, even though he couldn't explain what he actually did, have worked. The trauma the children have suffered hasn't been erased or wiped out, but they've somehow overcome it. Jez is more balanced and happier and is content to remain at the house, which is mostly to do with his relationship with Zafia. Bel has a new understanding of the world and is able to avoid Johnson and his gang. She has also found new wisdom and recognised that she needs to move away from the area, so she's got a transfer to another Better Futures home in Coventry. Jane is also healed and she too gets to move, to a home near the foster home where her sister lives. She has access to her sister now too, which they are both very happy about. And Danni is Danni, a jewel.

The Better Futures board incorrectly takes the moving on of these children as some sort of signal that Melanie's leadership is the wrong style for that home, so they dismiss her from the role. She thinks that maybe the writing was on the wall after the Alf incident. She's quite philosophical about it, especially after seeing the rapid improvements in the children; this has made it much easier to swallow and leave. There will be some continuity at the home, though, as Gemma is going to act as the interim manager.

Mike is given a positive send-off. Derek is worried, as Mike now doesn't have a job, but Derek decides not to press him to get one. *It's been a difficult time for us all, especially Mike,* he thinks. *I'll let him trundle on for a bit. I'm sure that's what my grandfather would have done in my position.*

Getting Even

78

Ted is a bit depressed by everything. He thought he was unflappable, but the lack of justice has hit him hard; it makes him feel like he doesn't matter. Mike, on the other hand, is now seething with rage.

'Ted, I looked up the guy who ran you over on Google. He is a baronet, Sir Sinclair Rufus de Courcy is his name,' says Mike. Ted nods but says nothing. Mike fills the silence with, 'What a wanky name.' Again, Ted nods.

Then out of his jacket pocket, Mike pulls the revolver that they used for the robbery. 'I know where he lives, and I'm going to go round and shoot the fucker. Are you coming?'

Ted looks worried. 'Hold on a second. This is a major thing to do and it wasn't on our bucket lists either.'

'It's bigger than that. It's top of a new list for me, something I call the fuck-it list. I'm sick of taking shit from people and I've had it with these types.'

Ted intervenes again, but his energy is lower than usual.

'I hear you, Mike, and I see you're angry, but let's not be so hasty.'

'I want action, Ted.'

'I'll tell you what then, let's visit the guy and explain the situation and see what he has to say for himself.'

Mike huffs, 'That's not action.'

'It is an action. It's us seeking clarity before one of us runs off and commits murder.'

Mike has a think. He reluctantly agrees.

'One other thing,' says Ted.

'What?'

'We won't bring the revolver with us. We're just going for a talk.'

With some agitation Mike responds, 'Fine, fine, I agree.'

79

They take a bus and then it's a twenty-minute walk to de Courcy's spread. Ted had suggested getting Ellen to give them a lift, but Mike said they weren't an item anymore and therefore it would be uncomfortable and perhaps inappropriate to make such a request of her. There are large concrete gate holders either side of the tall black steel gates that block the way into the de Courcy residence. There's an intercom on the wall next to the gate. Mike presses the button and it rings out. Eventually, a voice calmly calls out, 'Hello?'

In a mock-posh voice, Mike responds, 'Hello, how do you do? I am looking to speak with Sir Sinclair, please. I know him from the cricket and polo clubs.'

Ted pulls a face at his brother to say, *Well, look at you.*

The intercom voice responds, 'I'm really sorry, but Sir Sinclair is in Monaco at the moment and he isn't due to return for some time. But if you leave your details, I could organise a meeting with him over Zoom.'

Mike is annoyed. He lies: 'That's very kind of you, dear boy, I have his details; I'll just Zoom him myself. Or actually I'm due in Monaco myself the week after next; I'll go and meet him when I'm there.'

Ted pulls another face, that tells Mike he's impressed with his improvisation. The voice on the intercom says, 'Very well, thank you and good day.'

'Fuck this,' says Mike and then he climbs over the high wall. Once on the other side, he steps behind a tree. He looks around. He can't see any CCTV. Then he walks in an arc towards the side of the house where there aren't any windows; this is an attempt to decrease the chances of being seen.

He sees an outhouse. Initially, he thinks it's a stable, but once close and then inside, he appreciates that it's a garage where the cars are kept. There's a selection of cars. There's a Rolls-Royce, and he sits in it and makes a *vroom* noise while messing about with the steering wheel. There's a Porsche SUV of some kind and he just looks at it really closely and wolf-whistles at it.

Ted says, 'You're not your usual self. Let's just go.'

Mike ignores him and keeps walking around admiring the cars. 'In a while. I'm just looking, looking at how the other half live... well, I say half, but it's the one per cent, isn't it?'

'I think it's a fraction of the one per cent if you're referring to how people like the de Courcys live,' replies Ted.

Then Mike says, 'And what have we got here?' He is looking closely at a silver car and wolf-whistles again. Then he says to his brother, 'Have you not seen this car before?' But before Ted can answer, he answers for him: 'Of course you haven't, as you were hit from behind.'

Ted stares at the vintage Aston Martin and eventually cries out, 'Is this the car that killed me?'

'I believe so.' Having inspected it, he adds, 'And they've had it repaired. Look, not even a hint that it was involved in a crime, all spick and span again.'

'And I'm dead.'

Mike takes his house key from his pocket. He scratches the car all the way round, both sides, the bonnet and then across the boot. Then he inspects his handiwork and says, 'I can do better than that,' and this time he scratches the whole car in an anticlockwise direction.

'Thanks, Mike, you're a good brother,' smiles Ted.

Mike picks up a tyre iron. 'I'm not finished yet,' he says, and proceeds to break all the windows in the car. Then he throws the tyre iron on the ground and says, 'There, that's much better. Come on, let's get the fuck out of here.'

80

John Richards welcomes all ninety delegates back onto the course. There's a buzz of excitement. Different team members start to give their feedback. One team harassed women who were attending abortion clinics. The woman feeding back is very energised and uses lots of expletives and refers to those women attending the clinics as whores. Another group feeds back on how they hassled the children who were attending a Muslim school. At this, a number of people shout, '*Right on, well done,*' and there are some whistles.

A man tells of how his group kept disrupting an A&E department by constantly calling 999 and going into the department and setting off fire alarms. Another man explains how his group broke into a water treatment facility and opened pipes, which meant untreated sewage went into rivers. Some people challenge this, saying that it was a stupid thing to do, as most of the water companies are doing this themselves anyway.

After the break, John asks the teams to vote on the person within their team who's the best teammate, who has helped the team the most. Then the nominated fifteen are blindfolded.

John says, 'No peeking now. You'll be led into the next room, and you'll receive a prize.'

They are led through into a room where plastic sheeting covers the tile flooring. Then John walks everyone else into that space. He nonverbally explains to them what it is they are to do next. Many put on rubber gloves, and they reach into a number of now opened plastic bags and take handfuls of the substance within the bags. Then they offload this onto their fifteen blindfolded colleagues.

It's dog shit.

It's a frenzy. After about half a minute of this, John shouts out, 'Stop,' and then to the complaining fifteen, who have all taken off their blindfolds, 'Silence.'

Once there is quiet, he waits a few beats and then calmly, slowly and in a low voice says, 'The lesson here, right now, is that there are no teams. There is no best teammate. The lesson here is that you look out for number one, always and only.'

Then he shouts, 'And as for you fifteen, you super team players, you're just a bunch of losers. You're finished here. Now fuck off and don't ever come back.'

With that, John and the remaining seventy-five delegates return to the room they were previously in, and John closes the double doors behind him. Four of John's helpers stay in the other room, to escort the dog-shitty fifteen off the premises.

At the end of weekend two, John sets the seventy-five delegates more homework tasks which need to be reported on at the following weekend, weekend three.

Then there is more drama at weekend three, as twenty-five more people are expelled from the course. The remaining delegates are set more homework, which they need to feed back on during weekend four.

To everyone's surprise, no one is expelled on the final Saturday, and most of the final Sunday is a hot bed of toxic congratulatory antics, with all fifty being advised that they are no longer delegates but actual alumni of the Con Club. There is much cheering, with many taking great pride in referring to themselves as bastard masters and overlords of one kind or another.

81

Mike and Ted agree that it makes sense to text the number on the letter advising them to get in touch if they want to know more about what being a Tory really means. After a number of text exchanges, the guy, who is going by the name of Damian, suggests that they should meet up. They agree to do so in two days' time.

On the day, Mike and Ted head into the Grand Oak pub a minute before four p.m. There's no one in there apart from a barman. They sit at a table a bit away from the bar.

At a minute past four p.m. a man in his forties enters the bar. He looks around, scanning the area. He notices Mike and with a swagger makes his way over towards him. The man wears glasses, has long hair and is overweight, but not obese. He's wearing black boots, a green army coat and, underneath that, camouflage gear. Before he speaks, he looks over his shoulder, and then he says, 'You must be Mike?'

Mike nods and, extending his hand, says, 'Damian?'

The man shakes Mike's hand and says, 'No, no, I'm not Damian, I'm Geoff. Damian is running late. I've come along to help him out, but he is coming.'

Mike nods and asks, 'Are you army or ex-army, Geoff?'

Geoff shakes his head. 'No, no, I've never served. But I would if I was ever asked to, honest I would. Be in no doubt, I love my country.' He stands and places his hand on his breast and says, 'God save the King.' Then he sits back down.

'What's with the gear?' asks Mike.

'The gear? Well, money is tight, and I sometimes shop in the second-hand clothes stores, but you can get great deals in the army and navy surplus stores too, and I prefer these clothes, I feel more patriotic, so!'

Ted nods and so does Mike and they both say, 'Cool.'

'So, you want to know more about the Tories?' queries Geoff.

Ted nods and Mike says, 'Yes. We know a lot already, but we're a bit intrigued by what Damian has been saying, and we've had some recent experiences that have made us appreciate that there's more to the Tories than we first thought.'

'You've said *we* a few times; what do you mean by *we*?' Geoff asks.

'My family, my parents,' Mike qualifies whilst looking at Ted, who makes an annoyed face.

'Well, we, Damian and me, can certainly set you straight,' says Geoff, and then he takes some tobacco and papers from his pocket and starts to roll a cigarette while talking to Mike. 'The thing is, it all starts with education. Finland, now there's a system: no private schools, and as a result everyone in society focuses their energy on making all the state schools excellent. It's more balanced and fairer and meritocratic there. None of this class bullshit that has wrecked this country.'

Mike nods. Geoff continues, 'Thing is, here in England, the education system is deliberately set up to create splits. Private education makes up around seven per cent of the schooling in this country, but those seven per cent end up getting all the top jobs. Fifty to seventy per cent of all the judges, the media editors, the big finance CEO type jobs go to people from private schools. They protect themselves; they create a cycle, a system where those who have the money go private, and then hand down the top jobs to their kind and block the rest of society from getting a fair go.'

Mike interjects, 'But some people who don't come from money scrimp and save to go private, just to do the best for their children.'

'Yes, they do, because they know the system is rigged and it gives them a way in. Thing is, though, even then there's a hierarchy. If you're from money, you're viewed more positively. It's better to be an ankle-tapper within the seven per cent than to be a nobody as part of the other ninety-three per cent.'

Ted is listening intently, like Mike, but he isn't giving anything away.

Geoff puts the rollie in his mouth and is about to light the cigarette when Mike points to the sign.

'Sorry, I forget sometimes,' says Geoff. Then he continues, 'Don't tell me you haven't noticed? Think about it: how many of the people you know who went to private school are in good jobs, even if they aren't that bright?'

Ted turns to Mike. 'He has a point. There are lots of examples. They can all talk a good game, but when you scratch the surface, they aren't much to write home about.'

Geoff says, 'The system is rigged, totally rigged.'

Mike pipes up, 'So who are you and what do you do?'

Geoff nods. 'I'm woke.'

Mike looks confused and asks, 'What's woke?'

'Woke is about being anti-fascist, about being anti-corruption, about being for people, for equality. I'm a Tory too, but I'm from the more progressive, modern and liberal side of the party.'

Mike says, 'Same as my family then.'

Geoff continues, 'The Tories have always been a little bit anti-people and just about themselves – the donors and the party members, that is. But now, to be frank, it's just a toxic and far-right entity; they've purged all the moderates.' Again, Geoff goes to light his rollie, but he sees the sign of his own accord and stops.

Mike says with sincerity, 'I'm still a member of the party, and I hear what you're saying. I recognise the truth in all you've said.'

Then Geoff gets excited. 'France, now there's a country. They had a revolution and beheaded all the aristocrats; that's what we should have done. Man, we wouldn't have half the problems we have here now if we'd done that back then. No one messes with the working and middle classes in France.' He laughs as he makes a movement with both of his hands around his throat to signal a beheading.

Mike feels a little uncomfortable, but at the same time he visualises a scene where de Courcy loses his head. He looks at his watch. 'When should we expect Damian?' he asks.

'Very shortly,' says Geoff, and then sensing that he is losing Mike's attention, Geoff quickly pulls him back in. 'I went to Eton, you know. I've seen it all.'

Ted sits up straight and starts paying attention again.

Mike leans in. 'Really, when?'

Geoff leans in towards him and in a low voice explains, 'I was there recently, undercover, doing an exposé.'

'And what did you find?'

Geoff describes several scenes…

*

New students are arriving at Eton at the beginning of the year. In a very posh accent, a grey-haired man in a robe explains to the new students, 'What you are part of here is the biggest old-boy network in the country. You are here because you can afford it, and you can afford it because you're the best – the elite, the rulers, the owners of everything, the only people who matter.' The young people listen and take it all in. 'It's your job to rule. This is your birthright. You're from a different race.'

*

'It's break time now, boys. Take yourselves to the playground. Identify the weaker children and bully them mercilessly – dominate them. This is where the rest of your life begins.'

*

'Fuck public services, slim them down, figure out ways to plunder them. You have to master the blame game: blame the poor, the sick, the foreigners, especially the refugees.'

All the boys nod compliantly.

*

'Now I'm going to teach you to hunt. You can ride your

pretend horse and blow your pretend bugle. We haven't a fox, but I've got Rupert up from another year to play the fox. He's on a scholarship; he's poor.'

'My name is Robert, sir, not Rupert,' says the boy playing the fox.

The grey-haired man continues, 'I've told you before, whilst you're here, you're to be known as Rupert. Do you hear me, boy? You stupid ankle-tapper.'

Then another boy shouts out, 'Get that ankle-tapper! He isn't one of us; he's only here because of us needing to have ordinary folk here so we can keep our charity status. Let him earn his keep.' And then this aggressive boy blows his pretend bugle and they all chase after Robert.

*

A few grey-haired people in robes have gathered. One says, 'They keep saying equality, equality, take in different types, but that's against our very purpose.'

Another responds, 'Play the game. It's important for public perceptions. If we don't, we will end up having to take females.'

'Fuck that, dear boy,' says another.

Another pipes up, 'We have people here from different races and tiers of society already – the gardener, the catering staff, the driver. I really don't know what the problem is with these equality do-gooder types.'

*

A teacher is taking a history class. 'And you see, it was people like us, brilliant, exceptional types, who defeated the Jerries and ensured Britain won the war.'

A boy puts his hand up. 'I thought it was the Russians and the Americans who pretty much defeated the Nazis?'

'Don't be stupid, boy. Go see the headmaster immediately.'

*

Mike says, 'Christ, is it really like that? I'm more than shocked.'

Ted laughs and intervenes. 'Don't be believing any of that stuff. I've just been inside Geoff's head; he's never been to Eton. He's a bit delusional; he has mental health and addiction problems. You know Neal from the children's home? Geoff used to be friends with his brother before he died. Neal must have told Damian about you for some reason. Geoff isn't the brains of this outfit; he's Damian's cousin. Damian is the real deal. We just need to wait for him.'

Mike chills and then on cue, Damian arrives. He is tall, wearing a suit and walks confidently. Damian extends his hand. 'Hello, Mike, nice to meet you. You've met my cousin Geoff.'

'I certainly have.'

Damian gives Geoff some money and asks him to get some drinks from the bar. Once Geoff is out of earshot, Damian says, 'I love him dearly and am trying to help him out. He has a great imagination, and I can tell from your face that he may have told you some tales.'

'Yes, about Finland, the Tories, France and being at Eton.'

'Well, what he says about the Tories, France and Finland is usually true, but I'm not so sure about Eton. But it's because of Eton that I want to talk with you.'

'Go on,' says Mike.

'Have you ever read a book called *Dark Money* by Jane Mayer?' Mike shakes his head. 'What about *Posh Boys: How English Public Schools Ruin Britain* by Robert Verkaik?' Mike shakes his head again. 'You must; they're essential reading for you now. I do a lot of blogging and I write lots of articles for independent newspapers and websites on matters like corruption, like how the Russian state practically owns many in the Tory party et cetera. I really want to do a book on Eton in the style of Mayer and Verkaik, but I need an inside man.'

Mike looks confused. 'I know nothing about Eton. I can't help.'

'Yes, you can. You could get a job there.'

'I doubt it.'

'You could, as a tutor, especially now that you've had some experience working with children, at the children's home. They have a job going at Eton that you would be a perfect fit for.' Damian shows Mike an advert.

'That says physics. I know nothing about physics.'

'You did it at A level and touched on some of it during your computing degree; that will be enough to help you get by.'

'Yes, but it won't be enough for me to get selected. It says physics degree as an essential on the job specification.'

'I've thought about that. You'll have to apply as your deceased brother, Ted, and use his certificates.'

82

Ted likes the idea of checking out Eton. *'How bad can it be?'* *and 'It's not like we're doing anything else'* are some of the statements he's made to try to convince Mike it's worth doing. Mike's heart isn't in it, but Damian has given all of this serious consideration, so much so that he's got Neal to agree to be Mike's referee from the children's home and write the reference using the name Ted.

Mike eventually agrees. He applies for the job, is interviewed, and to his own surprise, is hired. Now he works at Eton, as Ted. He finds it nauseating. There is lots of elitism and constant reinforcement that the boys are extra special, the chosen ones, born to lead. Mike and Ted strongly agree that if the pupils didn't believe in societal hierarchies beforehand, they definitely do on the way out.

The only thing that the brothers feel really horrified by is regarding one of the guest speakers who comes to give a talk/lecture to the pupils. There are always speakers visiting, but Mike and Ted can't believe their eyes and ears with this one: the school has brought in a man who's well known for having far-right views, someone that many say is a fascist. The rhetoric and language used by this man energises and excites the pupils, so much so that slurs of profanity, racism and misogyny infuse the air and some of the pupils address schoolgirls who happen to be visiting from a state school at the same time in a vile way.

Damian is delighted to hear about all of this – not that he isn't appalled and sympathetic towards the girls, but this is perfect for his book. Another thing that Mike feeds back is that for a number of years most of the past pupils have gone on to work in the finance sector; not retail banks, but investment banks, hedge funds and private equity. Damian laps it up, but he isn't surprised; he knew this already.

He explains, 'The whole aristocracy idea hasn't gone away at all. Sure, it's not about land and estates anymore with everyone having to doff their caps to the lord of the manor because they rely on him for menial work or indeed a tenancy of some kind. But in reality, it's still there, just in a different form. How the money flows around is controlled by the elites, be that nationally or internationally. All the investments that are made, it's these people who either own the money or decide where it goes. Any entrepreneur with any decent ideas will have to get investment from them, and in this way the elites end up with major equity stakes in nearly every worthwhile idea that comes to market. The commoner or serf has never gone away, and they're always under the thumb. All that happens now is that the elites disguise everything; in fact, they're really, really good at that. Feudalism lives'

To a degree Mike believes what he is hearing because it aligns with what he's seen in life, but something about his facial expression makes Damian think that he isn't fully converted. 'I can tell you haven't read *Posh Boys* or *Dark Money* yet.'

Mike admits he hasn't, which leads to Geoff taking an unlit rollie out of his mouth and shaking his hairy head about whilst saying, 'For fuck's sake, read the books, man.'

Ted laughs at the cut of Geoff.

Damian is a busy beaver and has much of his book about Eton written. He is calling it, *How Eton Eats the People of the UK*. Mike, Geoff and Ted think it's a great title for the exposé.

83

While at Eton, Mike does some deep thinking. He tells Ted, Geoff and Damian that he's decided that once he finishes at Eton, he's going to become a Tory MP. Only from inside the party, he says, can he really try to turn back the tide and help drag the party back to being somewhere between the far right and right, as opposed to where it currently is, which is far-right and corrupt.

Any time he speaks of this, Geoff makes weird faces, as if he's constipated. Mike reads into this that Geoff isn't supportive of the idea, but Ted says that even though he's probably right in his analysis, there's also a good chance that Geoff is actually constipated. Mike agrees with Ted on this.

Damian does think it's a bad idea. 'You're wasting your time,' he tells Mike. 'They're a toxic bunch, beyond redemption. They're evil but with a little "e", or are at best are just short of evil.'

Mike listens to what they all have to say, and eventually Damian agrees to help him a little. Geoff stops making the strange faces and Ted steps away from being against the idea to just sitting on the fence, but he still isn't supportive of his brother's idea.

Damian advises, 'You'll need some serious contacts and connections to get this off the ground.'

'I agree,' says Mike, 'and I know just the person.'

But Mike isn't telling the truth, not even to Ted. He has become more and more lost in contempt for the man who killed Ted, de Courcy, and is hell-bent on revenge. He's thinking of killing him. He's googled him and given lots of consideration to how and where. Getting to de Courcy in Monaco isn't an option. He isn't in the UK much, and when he is, accessing him in an environment where Mike could take action against him would be very hard. However, if Mike were elected as an MP, he would definitely get access, as de Courcy is a big donor to the Tory party. All Mike would have to do is make out that he's philosophically aligned with de Courcy and the bear would come to the honey.

What a scandal, he thinks. *Tory MP kills Tory donor. Or maybe I don't even need to be an MP or win the party's vote to run at the next general election; maybe being a Tory nominee would be enough to get me near him.*

'Right, let me go and talk to someone I know who'll have connections,' Mike says. Then he adds, 'Thank you, Damian, and thank you too, Geoff. I gladly accept your support in this.'

The cousins look at each other with some confusion as they weren't offering to be part of Mike's election team at all.

84

Ted remonstrates with Mike. 'I don't want to meet Angelica. I don't like her.'

'I don't like her either, but needs must.' Ted frowns and Mike adds, 'It's not like she'll know that you're there, and you don't have to come if you don't want to.'

Ted bites back, 'And have you there on your own with that numpty Geoff? I think not.'

'I tried to shake him, but he thinks he's my campaign manager.'

Mike arrives at the wine bar ten minutes early and is surprised to see Geoff is there already. It looks like Geoff is taking this new role very seriously, as he has his wild long hair held back in a ponytail, and even though he's wearing his usual army regalia, he's trying to look more businesslike and is wearing a tie, a dark-blue one, which just looks wrong. Mike says nothing about his attire.

'So, your cousin has contacts?' says Geoff.

'Yes, well, she works in private equity, whatever that really is, and has relationships with different types of Tories to the ones we know, or so I'm led to believe.' Mike warns Geoff, 'She can be very cutting. She isn't like me or the rest of my family at all.'

Geoff nods and nervously plays with the three rollies he has on the table. Angelica is five minutes late and arrives wearing low-heeled shoes, a black knee-length skirt, a white blouse and a tan-coloured coat. She walks slowly but with purpose and a swagger. She air-kisses Mike on both cheeks and offers her hand to Geoff for a shake, but instead he inappropriately kisses it in a way he believes to be chivalrous, which makes Ted guffaw and then laugh uncontrollably.

'I'm intrigued to meet with you, Mike; you've captured my imagination. What is it you couldn't tell me over the phone?' asks Angelica.

Geoff intervenes: 'I'm his campaign manager. First things first, are you married?'

Angelica is surprised and looks like she is about to laugh, but whether that's because of Geoff's potential romantic interest in her or the fact he's just said he's Mike's campaign manager is unclear.

Ted laughs again. 'Actually, now I'm glad I did come. This is quite a show.'

Mike gives Geoff a look and, using his hands, gestures for him to cool it.

'So, how are you?' Mike asks his cousin.

'Good, thanks.'

'And what are you doing now?'

'I'm still working with the hedge fund.'

Mike makes sure he looks interested and Geoff follows his lead. Mike asks, 'And what do hedge funds do?'

Angelica sits more upright. 'Everything. Hedge funds and private equity own lots of things. It's about making money, investing, buying the right things and eventually selling them for the right price.'

'That's quite different to how my cousin Damian explains them,' says Geoff. 'He says they just buy companies, increase the fees the companies charge, cut wages, reduce the staff numbers, load debt and dodge taxes.'

Angelica laughs. 'Well, yes, we do that too.'

Then Geoff says, 'Could I get a job there?' No one is sure if he's being serious or joking.

'That depends. What is it that you do? Are you in the army?' she asks.

'No, no, I'm not, but if I was conscripted, I'd happily fight.'

Then she asks, 'Where did you go to school, Geoff?'

'See, Mike?' Geoff says. 'Damian was right: it's all about closed shops, private schools and elitism.'

Angelica laughs. 'Are you a lefty, Geoff?'

'No, yes, maybe.'

She laughs again. 'I don't know Damian or what he's said, but if you're implying that private schooling improves your chances of working in private equity, well, of course it does. The best-paying industries and the people who take charge of the capital flows and investments, have always been part of the ruling and elite classes, and their children always go to the private schools and because of their connections end up in the best jobs in the most important industries. That's why my father sent me private, so I'd get connected into that world. But even though I'm in, I'm not *in* in, if you know what I mean.'

Geoff nods. 'I know.'

Ted laughs. 'This guy is a whack job.'

Then Angelica addresses Mike. 'Dad said you changed careers and work for a children's home now. How noble of you. I looked up the company, Better Futures. You know, they're actually owned by a private equity company that's based in Panama.'

'What?'

'What do you mean by *what*?' asks Angelica.

'What do you mean Better Futures is owned by private equity based in Panama?'

'That's how private equity and hedge funds work. They buy other companies and organisations, and then restructure them, so they are controlled by a holding company, that they also own, which is always based offshore. That way they don't have to pay tax on any of the profits.'

Geoff takes the unlit rollie out of his mouth. 'It's all a scam. They don't pay a penny towards the running of the country, they don't contribute, not a penny towards education or the NHS. Damian is right, as are those books, *Posh Boys* and *Dark Money*.'

'No laws are being broken. It's all legal.' Angelica says calmly.

'Sure, but it's against the spirit of how businesses in Britain should be operating. Different rules for the rich, I see,' says Geoff.

'I don't deny that the rules are different for the rich; that's just how it is. And while they control big business and politics, the establishment will do what they always have. After all turkeys don't vote for Christmas, gents,' says Angelica.

'I don't work at the children's home anymore anyway,' says Mike.

'What are you doing now?'

'Nothing at the moment.'

In a proud way, Geoff adds, 'He was working at Eton.'

Mike wasn't going to say anything about that, so is caught off guard. Angelica has a look of incredulity and surprise on her face once she starts to realise that this is actually true.

'I was tutoring there for a while, and that's why I wanted to meet with you,' says Mike. Then he lies again: 'I was inspired by my time at Eton to such an extent that I've decided that I want to be an MP.'

It's now Angelica's turn to laugh uncontrollably; she gently removes tears from her eyelids using her well-manicured fingernails. 'You're both pulling my leg. Someone is going to jump out from behind a pillar with a camera now.'

The guys each keep a straight face. Then Geoff says, 'As I said, I'm his campaign manager.'

This completely triggers Angelica again, so much so that she puts her hand on her tummy to help prevent her from peeing herself with laughter. After she calms down, she says to Mike, 'I see you're serious, but it would be very hard for you to get the party nomination – not this quickly, that's for sure.'

'But we're all Tories, aren't we?'

'Yes, but there are different kinds of Tory and I don't think you're the kind that they like to have in place these days.'

'Fair enough, but would you at least try to help me?'

As she is considering this, Geoff puts a rollie in his mouth while offering her one from the table. She declines it with a shake of the head.

'I don't think anyone I know would be prepared to back you. But I do know how you could maybe come to the attention of, or make the acquaintance of, people with a say behind the scenes.'

'That would be great,' Mike says sincerely.

She advises him, 'You need to go to the Con Club.' Then she adds, 'Geoff, you'll love this. That book you referenced, *Dark Money*? Well, the Con Club is funded by an organisation that has charity status and an address on Tufton Street. It's a very right-wing organisation. Because it's registered as a charity, it doesn't have to declare where it gets its income from, but it's widely believed to be funded by a mixture of right-wing money from America and Russian state money that's coming in via some oligarchs.'

Geoff clenches his fists like he's just scored an FA Cup Final-winning goal – the ecstasy of validation. Ted looks quite worried; he doesn't think anything good can come from being connected to anyone in the Con Club. But Mike is pleased. He places his hand on Angelica's.

'Thank you, cousin. I knew I could rely on you.'

85

Mike and Geoff discuss all of this with Damian. He advises that he's heard all this before, and that the Con Club is rumoured to be financed by Russian money, dark money from the far right in America, and money from the oil and chemical industries too. The Con Club haven't divulged this, he says, because they don't legally have to. He also points out that their group rhetoric is aligned with the climate change deniers, the anti-abortionists and the pro-gun lobby. He's considering doing an exposé on the organisation for his next book after the Eton one, he says. He also tells them that he's heard lots of tales, unsubstantiated though, of preposterous things that have taken place at the Con Club, an almost cartoonlike style of behaviours at times.

Geoff, trying to big himself up, lies: 'I've heard that too.'

Damian says, 'That's how some parts of fascism have always behaved. It makes it feel like it's funny and surreal, and it's therefore more easily accepted. This is a common tactic you know. If something seems funny and surreal, people don't see it as a serious threat until it's too late.'

Mike says, 'You mentioned neoliberalism earlier. Is that not a good thing?'

‘It’s not. The fact that *liberalism* is part of the word makes it seem like it’s related to *liberal*, which is synonymous with freedom and goodness, but neoliberalism is almost the opposite of liberalism. It’s really about saying that you stand for extreme freedoms and total deregulation. In reality, that’s chaos and anarchy, the removal of rights for ordinary people and the enablement of total rule by the elites. It’s not about liberalism at all; it’s actually totalitarianism, something the autocrats, kleptocrats and dictators love. If you go there, Mike, you’ll need to be careful.’

Geoff takes the rollie out of his mouth and says, ‘We’ll be fine. I’ve read lots of articles about war and I did a taster day with the Territorial Army once.’

Ted starts laughing at Geoff again. Damian thinks Geoff’s statement is a bit insane, but he doesn’t want to mock his cousin or over-alarm Mike, so he keeps a straight face.

‘I hear you, Geoff, but even so, do take care. On a positive note, chaps, I’ve heard that some people who’ve attended the Con Club have ended up being headhunted to run as MPs in some constituencies, so your cousin might be right, Mike; maybe it will put you in the shop window.’

86

Mike and Geoff both get accepted onto the Con Club course, but once there, they sit apart from each other. Their plan is to act as if they're strangers. Both are wired with small cameras to record the proceedings in order to help Damian, who's said that he may do a documentary film as well as a book about the Con Club; he's as yet undecided. Again, John Richards is the main speaker and does all the introductions and most of the motivational speaking.

A woman catches Mike's eye. Her name is Vicki Sweeney. He can't explain it to himself or Ted; she just smiles at him and that's that, she's hooked him. She catches him looking at her twice, and he catches her looking at him once.

When the opportunity presents itself, Mike makes sure that he says things that are mildly racist. Ted isn't impressed, but Mike reminds him that he doesn't believe what he's saying but needs to speak this way to get noticed. Geoff wants to get noticed too and he is noticed, but for a totally different reason to Mike. Geoff starts talking to people about war and tells a story about the one day he spent in the Territorial Army. Everyone laughs. Most view him as a bit mentally unwell and very odd.

Again, everyone is divided into different groups. Mike ends up in the same group as Vicki. He's ecstatic. He is totally distracted by her and as a result doesn't pay as much attention to what's going on at the Con Club as he planned.

The following day, John Richards gives them all their tasks for the week ahead.

That night Mike says to Ted, 'I think I really like Vicki.'

'I think that was obvious to most people there.'

'Really? Shit, I was trying to play it cool. Do you think she twigged that I like her?'

'I'd say so,' says Ted. 'Your tongue hanging out was a bit of a giveaway.'

Mike slumps down. 'I'd never pull someone like her. She's way out of my league.'

'She is, but you never know, maybe you should chance it?'

'No, I'm too shy. I'd be too embarrassed by the rejection too. You know I haven't got the balls for stuff like this.'

'True, but I would if I was you.'

'Why? What do you know?'

'I had a peek inside her head. She likes you.'

'Really?'

'Yes, and I think she would say yes to a date.'

A delighted Mike asks, 'And what is she like, is she normal?'

'Normal enough. She had one really, really negative experience with an ex-boyfriend, an awful guy. I feel a bit sorry for her.'

'But she's an okay person and would say yes to me?'

'Yes, Mike, I told you already.'

87

The people in Mike and Vicki's group decide to split into mini teams, and Mike uses this as an opportunity to spend time with her. They decide that their project task will be to hack into the Labour Party website and change information relating to different MPs and shadow ministers to make them look really stupid and anal. This is done by the end of the Tuesday night, and Mike and Vicki celebrate by sharing a kiss.

'I think I really like you,' he says.

'I think I really like you too,' she says.

'God, this is really fucking boring,' says Ted.

Everyone returns on the second weekend. Just like before, each team feeds back on its exploits. Then they break, and after that John asks the teams to vote on the person within their team who was the best teammate, the person who helped the team the most. Then the nominated fifteen are blindfolded.

John says, 'No peeking now. You'll be led into the next room, and you'll receive a prize.'

Neither Vicki nor Mike were nominated, but Geoff was. Mike and Vicki don't throw excrement at anyone, and

Mike feels bad for Geoff. Ted doesn't laugh; he has a smirk on, though.

The seventy-five remaining delegates return to the other room. That's when Mike's jaw drops.

John Richards says, 'We've had some fun, but now it's time to get serious. I have a special guest I want to introduce to you. This person is a hero to me, someone who you should all look up to. He's a champion of the causes we believe in. Please, put your hands together for Sir Sinclair Rufus de Courcy.'

There is rapturous applause from everyone apart from Mike, who is concentrating hard; he does not take his eyes off the baronet. He doesn't even blink as he puts his hands around his waistband and then checks his inside pocket and his jacket pockets for the revolver. *Shit,* he thinks to himself, *I didn't bring it. But I can stab him with one of the steak knives at the break – no panic, that's what I'll do.*

88

De Courcy, overweight and puffy, is technically obese, but he isn't someone you would say looked particularly fat. 'A fuller figure' would be the polite way of describing his girth. He's wearing beige chinos, boat shoes, a white shirt and a navy jacket, all tailor-made no doubt.

'It's a pleasure to see so many brilliant like-minded people here today, people who see and think like I do, people who want to make a difference in this country. Some of you will want to step into the world of parliamentary politics, and I promise you, I will give you my full support and backing, so that we can ensure this country is run properly and for the people who matter. If the likes of us don't unite to shape party politics, the lily-livered will sell our party, our way of living, our country, all down the river. I am a great believer in low taxation or even no taxation. If the lowlifes of this country aren't smart enough to earn a living, why should we have to pay tax just so they can educate their offspring? Why should we have to pay for state schools? Fuck the chattel class.'

Mike cheers and claps. Ted finds this weird.

'If the lowlifes of this country aren't smart enough to

earn a living, why should we have to pay tax to fund their healthcare? They should be left to fend for themselves. We, their masters and superiors, shouldn't contribute a penny.'

Again, Mike cheers.

Ted says, 'What's got into you?'

Mike responds, 'Chill. I want him onside; that will get me a personal introduction, and once I'm close to him and away from his security detail, I'll completely fuck him up once and for all.'

This alerts and worries Ted.

De Courcy continues, 'They want a Robin Hood society where they do nothing but steal from the rich. Well, let them try. There are no more forests, so they have nowhere to hide; let them starve and rot on the streets.'

He spews bile for the best part of thirty minutes. Some of the delegates love this, but many appear uncertain, whilst others don't support this at all. Eventually, they all break for lunch. John Richards and de Courcy eat in a different part of the hall to everyone else. De Courcy's security detail remains standing nearby. Mike secretes a steak knife in his jacket. Ted sees this and is somewhat relived that de Courcy isn't near, and that the security person appears to be very alert and competent. However, this relief doesn't last long, as John approaches Mike.

'Mike, isn't it?'

'Yes.'

'Sir Sinclair has warmed to you. He'd like you to eat with us.'

Mike picks up his plate, John takes Mike's glass and these are repositioned just across from de Courcy, at the same table. De Courcy and Mike shake hands.

De Courcy says, 'I saw you were energised by what I was

saying.'

Mike says, 'I totally agree with you. You're completely right about everything.'

'John was telling me that last week you spoke passionately about the challenges of this country and the only real way to fix things.'

'Oh, I am passionate. I'm fuelled by revenge. I want people to get what they're due, get what's coming to them.'

'Too right,' shouts de Courcy.

Mike can see that the security detail isn't focused on him; his gaze is on the others in the room. John is sitting across from Mike too, to the right of de Courcy. Mike has his hand in his jacket pocket, tightly clasped around the steak knife. He looks across at his victim-to-be, who isn't wearing his jacket now, just a white shirt. Mike sees the area of the chest where de Courcy's heart is. He visualises the act. *All I have to do now is in one quick movement reach over and stick him with it. I should stab a few times until the security guy stops me. That should be enough to end this prick,* he thinks to himself.

Mike is ready – now is the time. He's about to take the knife from his pocket when Ted shouts at him, 'Stop, stop, don't do it! It wasn't him.'

Mike asks, 'What do you mean?'

'It wasn't him who killed me, it wasn't him who ran me down. He wasn't driving the car,' explains Ted.

'You're lying. You're just trying to stop me from doing this; you don't want blood on your hands. You've gone a bit chicken recently, haven't you?'

'Look, I'm not lying, I swear. Cross my heart and hope to die.'

Mike laughs, 'You're dead already, so you're really just

trying to manipulate me, aren't you?'

'Mike, I am not trying to manipulate you. Yes, I think killing a person right now and without fully thinking about it is wrong. But I'm not lying – he didn't kill me.'

A frustrated Mike shouts, 'Fine, but then who the fuck did?'

'There was another guy in the car at the time. He did it. Porky here was either blackmailed to take the rap or agreed to cover for the other chap; I haven't got that far yet. But from what I saw inside his head just now, it definitely wasn't him, I swear.'

Tying Up Loose Ends

89

That night Mike and Ted discuss what to do next.

'So, what you're saying is that the guy who was driving was de Courcy's son?'

'Yes.'

'And the father covered for the son, why exactly?'

'Well, there wasn't much time once you'd been knocked over, so the decision to swap places in the car was taken quickly. It was the son who manoeuvred the situation. He told his father that it was in the family's best interests that they swap seats; that another scandal involving him wouldn't be a good thing, and that de Courcy had been a shit and unsupportive father so should at least do one good thing for him in his life.'

'What a charmer. And what was the other scandal the

son was involved in?'

'Well, that Vicki Sweeney lady that you've started seeing… he was seeing her for a while. He did a lot of controlling things to her. She threatened to leave, so he beat her up and locked her in a log box on their estate. The police were involved, but favours were called in, and the Sweeneys accepted a pay-off.'

'And the son got away with it?'

'Exactly.'

Mike thinks for a few moments and says, 'Well, let's find him. I'll shoot him with our great grandfather's gun.'

'Look, let's pause on all this killing for now. I think we should definitely find him. I'll have a look inside his head and see what's been going on. Then we can reconvene, and then if we both agree that he should be dispatched, we'll plan it properly.'

Mike quickly says, 'Agreed.'

'In that case, I know where he is. He's staying at the de Courcy estate right now.'

No time like the present, they agree, so later that night they make their way to the de Courcy place. Obviously, they've been there before, and they don't bother ringing the intercom as they want to enter without being noticed.

They climb over the outer wall and head to the back of the mansion house. They try a few doors, but these are all locked. They notice a partially open window on the first floor which can be accessed via the flat roof of a single-storey annexe building. Mike climbs up onto this and is able to get into the house.

He doesn't know the layout of the house or who is in which bedroom, but when they were looking for a way in, he noticed that on the ground floor a couple of lights were on and there was some music playing at a low volume. Therefore, it makes sense to head there first, and this turns out to be a good decision. Because it's in the drawing room that they find Boniface Jeffrey Mervyn de Courcy, the third-born son of the baronet and the man who actually ran Ted down.

Ted goes inside his head right away. After ten minutes he comes back out. Ted appears a little different on his return, as if he's a bit traumatised by whatever he's just seen, but this is to be expected, as the mind of the person who killed him is certainly a strange place to have been.

Mike asks, 'Are you alright?'

'No, I'm not.'

'Let's go home then.'

Ted shakes his head. 'No, let's not. I can't handle home right now.'

'Fine,' says Mike, and they depart and head to a budget hotel.

90

The following day, Ted wakes way before Mike does. Ted uses this time to think.

'Morning,' says Mike.

'Morning,' replies Ted.

'So, are we going after Boniface?' asks Mike.

Ted waits before responding and then asks, 'Do you trust me?'

Mike sits up and has a think, and then replies, 'Yeah, you're probably the only person I trust.'

'Okay then, let's wait till Saturday and we can set the ball rolling when we get to the Con Club.'

Saturday arrives. Everyone turns up at the Con Club as planned, but before the process to reduce the number of delegates from seventy-five to sixty commences, Mike approaches John Richards.

'John, there's something I want to share with you.'

'What's that?' asks John.

'Look, it's hard for me to put this into words and it's even harder for me to explain how I can make you aware of what it is I want to make you aware of, but I need your permission to put my hand on your shoulder and keep it there for a short while. If you allow me to do this, I promise you, you'll receive visuals from me that will be of serious interest to you.'

John looks perplexed, but he has nothing to fear. He is ex-military, served with the SBS, the Special Boat Service, and survived the injuries he received from an IED in Afghanistan. He can certainly survive some weirdness from Mike.

Mike puts his hand on John's shoulder, allowing Ted to make his way into John's ear. Ted has been in there before, on the first weekend, which is why he knew he needed to get back in there again. Not only is Ted able to read people's minds and heal them, but he also has another ability too: he can replay other people's memories inside someone else's head. And what he wants to show John Richards is what Boniface de Courcy has done.

From his previous excursion inside John's head, Ted knew that John had suffered badly from his injuries in Afghanistan, more mentally than physically. He suffered depression and became addicted to alcohol. His sister Louise had been a rock for him and helped him get through everything. He has been on the dry for years now. He got what he considers to be a soft job, at the Con Club, through a mate of a mate, and it suits him, even though he doesn't believe in half the shite he has to spout, and almost none of the shite he hears.

When Louise died, John was devastated. Louise had her own struggles at different times in life and had been known to self-harm. She would cut her arms or burn herself, but she was never suicidal. Then she got into a relationship with Boniface, and Boniface would be a terrible partner for anyone, as Vicki could attest, but to someone with Louise's vulnerabilities, he was soul destroying. He psychologically and emotionally fucked her up. And he got a huge kick out of it. Ted wants to show this to John and he does. But there's something else.

In her desperation to be loved, during one of their arguments, which was instigated by Boniface's toxic behaviour, Louise placed a needle attached to a syringe containing a very high dose of heroin into a vein in her left arm. 'I'll do it, I'll do it, I swear, I'll do it, I'll overdose,' she cried.

Boniface shouted at her, 'I doubt it very much, you waste of space. I've had enough of you. You aren't the only one I'm fucking either, but you sure are the most boring.'

Louise cried some more. 'I will do it.'

There was to-ing and fro-ing like this for a number of minutes and then Boniface finally sneered at her, 'Let me help,' and he pushed the plunger to the end of the syringe, and without any resistance from the broken Louise, the heroin entered her bloodstream. Then he fucked off and left her to pass from this world into the next.

Ted makes his way back out of John's head. John doesn't move. He's in shock. He stands like a statue for about five minutes, and then says to Mike, 'Thanks for sharing that,' and walks out of the room. He goes to one of the hotel's bars and asks for a pint.

'Of what?' asks the barman.

'Vodka,' is John's response.

The barman smiles because he thinks John is cracking a joke. Eventually, the barman realises that John is being serious and he serves him a whole pint of vodka.

John hasn't let a drop touch his lips in seven years and the vodka is downed very quickly. He has a sandstorm of thoughts, but at the centre of all this is one thing and one thing only: anger. He will have his revenge. *Fuck Boniface and fuck the elitist pricks like him.*

He returns to the main room and addresses the seventy-five remaining delegates. Calmly, he says, 'Ladies and gentlemen, let me set you your next task.' He slowly paces about at the top of the room. 'How do you think the people you wish to emulate became who they are today? How do you think any of these well-to-do people got what they have?'

There is a lot of thinking going on in the room. Then, with more energy, John continues, 'I'll tell you. Many of them inherited it, but whether they come from new money or old money, at some stage it came from someone reaching out and just taking it from someone else. That's what they did: they grabbed it from someone else, usually with force. In blood sometimes, and almost always illegally. What do you expect? If you want to join the part of society that the rule of law doesn't apply to, then you have to break some laws to gain entry.'

Then he shouts passionately, 'Get out there, show them that their time is up, let them know that you're ambitious, send them a message. Your future begins now. Make it happen.' And as they all energetically leave the venue, he shouts after them, 'I'll see you next week.'

Mike has no intention of going on a rampage. While all this was going on he couldn't stop staring at Vicki. Ted is very clear that he still doesn't want to go home, and Vicki takes Mike up on his offer, which is, 'Let's go to yours.'

91

Mike spends much of the week at Vicki's and the news is full of stories of rich people, some of them titled, some of them in the money districts of London, being attacked. Some have their houses trashed and their cars burned. No one is killed, but there are injuries.

Three men from one Con Club team are apprehended by the security team of an intended victim and arrested by the police. In custody the men say nothing apart from the slogans they learnt on the course from John, de Courcy and others. They interpret being arrested as part of the game and believe that they need to ensure they come across as in control and entitled, or they won't pass the test and won't get in.

John goes after Boniface. Ted knew he would. John is able to open a back gate into the de Courcy estate and drive right in. He parks the Jeep he's stolen a little bit away from the main house so as not to wake anyone. He's dressed in black and is wearing a balaclava.

He breaks into the house and comes across his victim. Boniface is already drunk, but John injects him with something to ensure he won't resist, and then he guides him to the Jeep with hands-on support. He ties him up and tapes his mouth. Then he lays him on the floor in the back of the Jeep.

John drives to an isolated safe house in the middle of nowhere and ties Boniface to a chair in an outhouse. He leaves him there for a day. Then he reveals his identity to Boniface and starts to work on him. Initially he'd planned to torture and kill Boniface, but then he changed his mind. He still tortures him – psychologically, though, not physically. And of course, he has to rough him up occasionally.

First John gets a videoed confession from Boniface regarding Louise's death, and then a written one. He knows there's a chance that once in front of the police, Boniface will deny the confession or say it was forced, and as a result it may never reach court. But he also knows that Boniface knows who and what John is and was, and that John is someone who will keep his word. He threatens Boniface, saying that if he doesn't take what's coming to him legally, then John will come back for him and kill him. Maybe up close, a dagger to the heart, or maybe he'll slip him a deadly neurotoxin, or maybe he'll just blow his head off with a high-powered rifle from a safe distance. As dangerous and damaged and selfish as Boniface is, he's also no fool. He knows he's not in John's league and that he has to take his words seriously.

John carefully drops the confessions off at a police station, and then he goes back for Boniface. He strips him, ties him to the front of the Jeep, throws water over him and then drives him down the motorway at over a hundred miles per hour for about ten minutes, before parking the Jeep in front of a different police station to the one the confessions were delivered to.

He leaves Boniface tied to the bonnet. His final words to him are, ‘Please, please retract the confession. Please. And I’ll pay you another visit, a final visit. Bye for now.’ And then he disappears.

92

Following on from all the Con Club antics on the news, Damian starts to phone and text Mike. He doesn't take the calls but does respond via texts. Without going into details or giving the game away, he confirms that at the Con Club that weekend things took a serious turn for the worse.

Mike eventually agrees to meet up with Damian once he and Vicki come up for air. He goes to the pub they normally meet in, and even though he's ten minutes early, both Geoff and Damian are there already. Damian is very eager. Mike tells him pretty much everything apart from the aspects of the story involving Ted.

Damian, deep in thought, nods. 'So for no obvious reason, John Richards flips and instructs the delegates to run riot?'

'Yes,' says Mike.

Then an animated Ted shouts at Mike, 'Tell him no more, nothing! He isn't on our side anymore; he's a fucking turncoat. Ask him about the book.'

A confused Mike shrugs his shoulders and turns to Damian. 'How's the book?'

Damian's tone changes. 'Good, thank you.'

'Bullshit,' says Ted. Then he directs his brother to say:

'When will it be out?'

Damian sheepishly says, 'Not for a while, unfortunately. I ran into a little snag with the publishers.'

Geoff starts to look a little upset for his cousin as he didn't know this.

'Fucking liar,' shouts Ted. Then he instructs his brother, 'Just say what I say.'

Mike says, 'I heard different.'

Damian again looks sheepish and Geoff starts to twig that something is up.

Mike continues, 'I heard that you withdrew the book; that there was a publishing deal in place and it was ready and good to go to market and, but you withdrew the manuscript.'

'What?' says Geoff.

Damian makes noises but is a bit stuck for words, so Mike continues.

'You did a deal with bloody Sinclair Rufus de Courcy. He has the rights to the book now – isn't that true?'

An incredulous and irritated Geoff calls out his cousin, 'Damian, Damian, tell me this isn't true?'

Damian sits tight, saying nothing. Then he confidently states, 'What Mike has said is correct.'

'Is this motherfucker blackmailing you or something?' shouts Geoff. 'Because I have contacts in the Territorial Army who can sort him out. Just say the word.'

'No, I'm not being blackmailed.' Damian pauses before adding, 'De Courcy made me an offer I couldn't refuse.'

Geoff is confused. 'But that Eton exposé was something we worked on for years.'

Damian gently corrects him: 'Something I was working

on.'

Mike chips in, even though Ted knows the answer to the question already. 'What was the deal?'

'De Courcy owns a number of newspapers and magazines. He offered me a large salary, and I'm now the editor of *The Only Way*.'

The Only Way is a well-known weekly magazine.

'That's a right-wing rag,' shouts Geoff, and he grabs his cousin by the lapels and starts to shake him. 'I've been trained to kill, you know!'

Damian breaks away and pats down his clothes. 'We all know you haven't been trained in anything apart from making rollies, Geoff.'

An emotional Geoff calls out, 'You've sold out.'

'I have not. What I've done is *buy in*.'

'You've sold out, because we aren't like his lot.'

'We're all Tories, Geoff. If anything, I'm just more of a Tory now,' says Damian.

Mike is as aghast as Geoff, who is deflated and crestfallen and sits back down. Ted has been waiting for the right time and now he instructs Mike again to say exactly what he is told.

'Bravo, Damian,' Mike says, 'you're totally right. An exceptional piece of business by you.' Mike continues, 'It's inspired really. I'm so impressed with you. I knew you had something about you… well, you had, but you have more about you than I first understood. I think we should celebrate.' And he calls out to the barman, 'A bottle of champagne, please.'

Damian is onside, so Mike continues, as instructed by Ted: 'I'm happy to be working for you and with you, and if you're the main man at *The Only Way* now, then I'll support you on this venture too.'

A pissed-off Geoff says, 'Fuck this,' and leaves. Mike wants to say and do the same, but instead he stays seated and continues to tell Damian everything Ted says.

'Don't worry about Geoff, he'll come round. It might take him a week or two, but he will.'

93

Mike heads to a hotel for the evening, and stays there for the following day and evening too. Ted is still insisting that they don't go home, and Mike isn't in the mood to stay at Vicki's. Also, he needs to speak with Ted, to figure out what Ted is up to and why the hell he's now so aligned with Damian.

At the hotel Mike says, 'So, explain.'

Ted does. 'Look, I'm as pissed off as you and Geoff. In a way, what Damian has done is what always happens. Everyone has a price. He's been bought off. I mean, what are Tory values, Mike? What the fuck are they? I would love to kick Damian's ass, but what I see is an opportunity.'

Mike has been listening intently. 'And what is that?'

Ted continues, 'You, we, have been invited to a media event the day after tomorrow with Damian, because we're now with *The Only Way*. That's what I was angling for.'

Mike is unimpressed. 'An event? So what!'

Ted gets serious. 'It's an annual event, and each year the prime minister attends. I'm going to sort out the prime minister.'

'Whoa, what do you mean, sort out?'

‘Nothing bad. Chill, Mike. I’m just going to get inside his head.’

‘To do what?’

Ted explains, ‘There’s so much bad politics. There’s so much that’s rotten about our party. I want to get in there and use my powers to shape him up, to get him to say and do positive and meaningful things, to bring some balance to the party and to the country, to get him to do things that are right and proper and that benefit the many and not just the few.’

‘And you think you can do that?’ queries Mike.

‘Yes.’

‘Okay, in that case, I’ll help you. I expect what you’ll want from me is to get you as close to the prime minister as possible, so you can get onto his shoulder and then into his ear.’

‘Exactly,’ says Ted.

94

Security is tight for the event, but Mike gets through easily enough as he's been vetted and is one of many media people there. Damian is making use of his newfound status as he mingles with the high and mighty.

Mike sees the prime minister. He is working the room, or so it appears. What he's really doing is mingling with Tory party donors only. Mike tries to make his way towards him, but it's not going to be so easy. He can't just barge into the group that the prime minister is part of.

Ted sees the direction that the prime minister is moving in; it's clockwise. He spies a couple of extremely well-known Russian oligarchs. Ted tells Mike to go and talk to the Russians. He does, and it pays off as the prime minister comes over to them to say hello. He addresses the Russians by their first names and shakes their hands, and before he starts to converse with them, he looks at Mike's ID badge, which says his name and the name of the magazine. The prime minster taps Mike on the arm, uttering, 'Good job, good magazine.'

Mike uses this as an opportunity. He reciprocates the gesture, tapping the prime minister's arm, whilst saying,

‘Thank you, Prime Minister. You’re truly brilliant.’

This is all Ted needs. Having anticipated Mike’s action, he makes his way onto the prime minister’s shoulder. From there he climbs up to the outer ear. He slips inside the eardrum with his usual ease, so he can get near to the stirrup, and this is when he freezes. He’s shocked, caught off guard; he didn’t expect to see what he’s seeing.

There are two other tiny people there already. One is clearly a security person and the other is grey and elderly. The elderly man… Ted can’t place him initially, but then twigs who he is. He’s a far-right multi-billionaire American industrialist, and he has his hand on the prime minister’s stirrup and is uttering, ‘Fuck the people, fuck the people, fuck the people.’

Ted doesn’t know what to do, but then the elderly man spies Ted and orders his bodyguard, ‘Get him.’

The security guard runs at Ted and punches and kicks him. Ted is taking a beating and the guy has him pinned down, but as the guy reaches into his pocket for something to tie Ted up with, Ted takes his opportunity. He kicks up at the guy and then quickly gets to his feet. He slips round the eardrum and runs out of the outer ear as fast as he can and jumps onto the prime minister’s shoulder. From there he jumps onto a different person entirely. The security guy from inside the ear doesn’t follow.

Ted catches his breath resting on the shoulder of this stranger. Then he calls out to Mike, who starts a conversation with the stranger, and him moving closer to this person, enables Ted to get back onto home turf, Mike’s body.

‘You weren’t in there that long, Ted. Did you achieve the objective?’

Ted shakes his head. 'No, I couldn't, but I now know two major things that I didn't know before.'

'What's that?'

'I now fully understand why the Tory party only support the rich and fuck everyone else over, and I know that I'm not the only one-centimetre-tall person in the world – somehow there are others.'

He explains the details to Mike and says they might as well leave now, as there isn't anything more that they can do there today. Mike suggests they head home, but Ted is still reluctant to go there.

Home Sweet Home

95

Ted eventually agrees that they should go home. He has been putting it off. Once they get home, Mike checks on his mum. She's asleep on the floor of the kitchen with a blanket over her. There's an envelope on the table with Mike's name and address on it. Inside is a letter and a photo. The picture is of Elton John, and written on it is a message: *Hello, Gertrude, I hear you're a huge fan, best wishes, Elton.* The note says:

Dear Mike,

My lawyer was told by the police that the reason you were hassling me was to get a signed picture for your mum, and that you'd had a family tragedy recently where your brother Ted died. You should have said. Please find what you were looking for inside the envelope. I still don't want to see you again, though.

Best wishes,

Elton

'How cool is he!' says Ted.

'Ice cool,' says Mike. 'Mum will be delighted.'

Then Mike heads into the sitting room. Derek is there. They exchange pleasantries. Derek is watching the news, a story about the prime minister vomiting at an event.

Ted says to Mike, 'That happened when I was being assaulted by that guy inside the PM's ear.'

Mike nods in agreement.

'So, son, how are you?' asks Derek.

'Okay, I suppose. I have a new girlfriend.'

'That's great. And what are you doing for work now?'

'I'm in between jobs now. I was at the children's home, as you know, then I worked at Eton for a while, and recently, well, for a couple of days I was with a magazine.'

'You're still young. You'll find a career that you like,' Derek says.

Then Mike notices Ted. He hasn't been around for a few minutes but now he is again, and he's sobbing.

'What's wrong, Ted, why are you so upset?'

Ted continues to cry. 'I don't know whether I should tell you or not.'

'We're brothers, we have no secrets.'

'There's a reason I haven't wanted to come home for a while. I was afraid that what I found out would end up being true.'

Mike smiles. 'What are you on about, little brother?'

Ted continues to cry and then he starts to explain. 'I've just been inside Dad's head.'

Mike queries this: 'But you said you would never go inside our parents' heads?'

Ted continues to sob. 'I did, and I wish I hadn't had to.'

'And?'

Ted offloads: 'Sir Sinclair de Courcy, he had long-standing wealth, and it was his third son, Boniface, who killed me. The thing is with Boniface, what I understood from being inside his head is that if he'd been the second son, he would have killed his eldest brother to inherit his father's estates, but because he's the third and would have to kill two elder brothers, he won't do it. He doesn't think he'd get away with it. But Boniface has always been looking for ways to prove himself and make his own wealth, and eventually he got lucky.

'During the Covid lockdowns, Boniface set up a number of companies to supply PPE. You will recall, the government didn't use the professional outfits that historically supplied PPE. They used the pandemic as an opportunity to enrich their backers as much as they could. Boniface benefited greatly.

'The thing is, I was really pissed off about all of this; it was an emotional time. I was writing lots of letters to local Conservative Party members complaining about it, Tweeting and doing stuff on Facebook too. At the time I had no idea Boniface existed. But he knew about me, I was annoying him. Annoying him enough that he researched me.

'Through the Chamber of Commerce, Dad heard that the government were giving out PPE contracts, so he set up some companies, but he wasn't getting anywhere. He was advised to make contact with Sinclair de Courcy and to win his support. It was well known that the baronet was involved in some of the decisions as to who was getting these big-money deals. Dad went round to see him, but he was in Monaco. However, he did meet Boniface.

'Boniface berated and manipulated Dad. He told him that he was being blocked from getting contracts because of me. He told Dad he'd missed out on millions because of what I'd been doing and showed him the stuff on Facebook and Twitter and some of the letters I'd written. Boniface told Dad that only if he agreed to me being taught a little lesson would Sinclair intervene, take Dad off the blacklist and get him onto the agreed list. That's why I'm upset, Mike. I saw this inside Boniface, and I've just seen the same inside Dad.'

This is a lot for Mike to get his head round. After a couple of minutes, he turns off the TV. 'Dad, were you involved in Ted's death?'

A guilty-looking Derek says, 'What do you mean? Of course not.'

'Dad, don't lie to me. You were. I know all about the PPE and Boniface de Courcy.'

A tear starts to form in Derek's eye. He pauses and composes himself. 'Things happen in life that you don't expect, son. I thought I'd have a different life. I thought I'd make it as an accountant and it never happened; things got in the way. I thought things would be different with your mum, but she has her demons. I love being part of the Conservative Party, but even so, I didn't make it big there either. I'm in there, but I'm not really in.

'I saw the whole PPE thing as an opportunity to make some money. The government were dishing out huge contracts to anyone connected to the party; no experience in PPE or procurement was required. It was just a get-rich-quick scheme. But I wasn't getting anything from them, even though I was pushing hard.

'I went to see the baronet and ended up meeting Boniface. He said the reason I wasn't getting anything was Ted. He said if I agreed to Ted being taught a little lesson, then the millions would start to flow in my direction. I agreed. Then time passed, and I still didn't get any deals. But nothing happened to Ted either. Then there was less happening with PPE.'

Crying now, he continues, 'When Boniface said "a little lesson", I thought he meant a few punches or something. That's what I thought I was agreeing to.'

Ted has been crying throughout. Then Gertrude rushes into the kitchen. She has been listening. She's in a tearful rage. She runs at Derek, who remains seated, and she slaps him across the face a number of times before running back out of the room.

Derek says to Mike, 'I deserved that.'

Then Gertrude returns to the sitting room and walks back up to Derek. She is crying and uses her left hand to wipe away her tears and to get her hair out of her eyes. In her right hand she's holding the revolver.

Simultaneously, Ted, Mike and Derek shout, 'No!', but she shoots Derek in the forehead at point-blank range. He dies instantly.

She immediately drops the gun and runs over to the sofa and lies down and cries uncontrollably.

Mike and Ted are stunned.

'Fuck,' says Mike.

Ted has stopped crying. 'This is so fucked up,' he says. Then he asks, 'What are we going to do?'

'I don't know. Mum will go to jail for this,' says Mike. Then he follows up with, 'She won't remember this. She's so pissed, you know, that I could take the blame, say it was me.'

'And go to jail?'

'I'd go on the run.'

'You wouldn't survive a day.'

'I'd need help, but I know a guy.'

'Who? Geoff?! Get a grip,' says Ted.

'No, John Richards. I have his number.'

'You're sure about this?'

'I think so.'

Mike gets out his phone and dials John's number. Someone picks up and says hello. The man doesn't identify himself, but Mike knows it's John.

'Hello, it's Mike. I've got a problem: my mother just killed my father. I'm going to take the blame for it, but I need to go on the run as I can't do prison. Can you help?'

John says, 'Life is really shit sometimes. I can. I need to get rid of this phone and number now. If you want help, I'll collect you in thirty minutes.' He gives the coordinates of a meeting place to Mike. 'I'll wait five minutes. If you don't show, I'll assume you changed your mind or you've been caught.'

That's the end of the call. Neither brother says anything for a minute and then Ted has a flash of brilliance. 'We could dress it up as suicide. It was at point-blank range; the gun was virtually on his forehead. You wipe the prints off, put Dad's on, and tell the police he did it himself.'

'What about the blood splatters on Mum?'

'We can say she tried to stop him, and that was why she was so close and got splattered.'

'It won't work. She'll say she shot him.'

Then Ted has another idea. 'I could go inside Mum's head and wipe this memory from her, and fix her, make her well, while I'm in there too.'

With excitement Mike says, 'That's a great idea. Let's do that.'

Ted waits before going into his mother's ear. 'The thing is, I haven't told you everything about my condition.

Reading people's minds uses up energy, but helping them uses up quite a lot of energy too. My life force is a lot less than it was, my energy levels are less. I think that there's a real chance that if I go into her ear and fix her, then I won't return; that my energy will be totally used up and gone, and so will I.'

Without hesitation, Mike immediately tells Ted, 'Under no circumstances do you go in there. Do not help her. I love her, but you mean more to me. I've become so close to you over the past few months; you're the most important person in my life now.'

'Same,' says Ted. He looks at his brother and then his mother, and then he says, 'Oh, fuck it.'

Mike shouts 'No!' at him, but Ted heads inside his mother's ear and makes his way to the stirrup bone.

Five minutes later, Gertrude sits up. She's sober, she's relaxed. She sees Mike. 'Hello, darling.' She gives him a hug and then sees her dead husband. 'Oh my God! What happened?'

Mike explains, 'He shot himself. You tried to save him; that's why you have blood splatters on you.'

'I remember. Poor Derek,' she says. Then she adds, 'We need to phone the police.'

She makes the call. Mike has a look around for Ted, quietly calling out his name. Mike doesn't notice his mum ending the call and she sees him calling out Ted's name. She reaches over and hugs him again. 'Oh honey, I know this is a lot to take in. We lost poor Ted too. I understand that you miss him.'

Then she breaks away from the hug as something else has caught her attention. She walks towards an object leaning against the wall. 'What's that picture doing down there?'

'Dad did that ages ago,' Mike explains.

She picks the picture up and places it back on the wall. It's a picture of Margaret Thatcher. 'There,' she says. 'I do love Maggie.'

Mike turns to his mum. 'Yes, you said that before,' while thinking to himself, *Fuck, I thought Ted fixed her. Too many just don't understand that if it wasn't for Thatcher and a whole load of others, things wouldn't be as fucked up as they are today for most people. There's something seriously wrong with us Tories.*

96

Gertrude takes charge of Derek's funeral arrangements. One of the main differences between this one and Ted's is that the Elton John songs chosen for Derek's are upbeat: '*I'm Still Standing*' and '*Crocodile Rock*'. Initially, people think these are inappropriate, but Gertrude is positive and confident and is using the event to showcase positivity towards Derek, and people generally shrug their shoulders and join in the groove.

Mike's singular contribution to the event has been in choosing the funeral director; he insisted on giving the gig to Mark Hillier. Mike's only anxiety centres around the cremation. He's worried. He hasn't seen Ted for two weeks now, so he's starting to accept that he's totally gone, but he's anxious that what happened with Ted might happen with his dad too, that some version of him might return. But he doesn't.

THE END

Thank you to Charlie, Damien, Jackie, Rose and Steve.

And a thank you to Claire Keegan too, who I have never met. If she hadn't written *Small Things Like These*, which I haven't read yet, I may not have bothered to sit down and write *The Con Club*.

Printed in Great Britain
by Amazon

36611168R00145